RANDY PITKIN

Restored

From Brokenness and Trauma to Wholeness and Peace

First published by Independantly published 2024

Copyright © 2024 by Randy Pitkin

All rights reserved. No part of this publication may be reproduced, stored or transmitted in any form or by any means, electronic, mechanical, photocopying, recording, scanning, or otherwise without written permission from the publisher. It is illegal to copy this book, post it to a website, or distribute it by any other means without permission.

Randy Pitkin asserts the moral right to be identified as the author of this work.

First edition

Cover art by Ryan Hoebbel

This book was professionally typeset on Reedsy. Find out more at reedsy.com

*This book is dedicated to God and His Son.
Without His mercy and grace, I would not still be here.
To Felicia, my guardian angel, who has never left my side.
To Andrew and Randee, my legacy.*

*"Children begin by loving their parents.
As they grow, they judge them.
Sometimes they forgive them."*
Oscar Wilde

Contents

Foreword	iii
Preface	iv
Acknowledgments	vi
Introduction	1
Chapter 1	7
That's Life	7
Chapter 2	21
That's the Way of the World	21
Chapter 3	27
Foolishness of Youth	27
Chapter 4	46
Movin out	46
Chapter 5	58
Atlantic City	58
Chapter 6	76
I Will Always Love You	76
Chapter 7	104
Losing my Health and More	104
Chapter 8	112
House of the Rising Sun	112
Chapter 9	121
Break the Man	121
Chapter 10	151
Sowing the Seeds of Love	151

Epilogue 170
About the Author 184

Foreword

"People raised on love see things differently than those raised on survival" Joy Marino

I was raised on fear and did not see the love that was there all along. God's love and then my wife's. This is my journey from darkness to light. From brokenness to wholeness. I masked the pain and brokenness with sex, drugs and alcohol. This is a tale of self-discovery, Enlightenment, Spirituality, Healing and Wholeness. It's my hope that my story may bring healing to others still bound by their past.

"Some time later, Jesus went up to Jerusalem for one of the Jewish festivals. Now there is in Jerusalem near the Sheep Gate a pool, which in Aramaic is called Bethesda and which is surrounded by five covered colonnades. Here a great number of disabled people used to lie—the blind, the lame, the paralyzed. One who was there had been an invalid for thirty-eight years. When Jesus saw him lying there and learned that he had been in this condition for a long time, he asked him, **"Do you want to get well?"** **(John 5:1-6 NIV)**

Preface

This image is an example of **Kintsugi**. In Japanese culture, a broken item can be repaired and made more valuable by repairing it with gold. Notice the cracks are not hidden. They are still there but the gold holds it all together and adds value. Our own cracks, scars and imperfections make us who we are. They are a part of our journey. But they do not have to define who we are in the future. Once repaired we are useful for whatever purpose life has in store for us. We don't throw away people who are damaged. We repair them.

"Kintsugi"

Acknowledgments

To all who have ever loved me and believed in me, I have never forgotten you. Thank you for your love, friendship and support.

Introduction

It was a Thursday morning in September, the Seventh to be exact, in the year 1961. I was born at Grace New Haven Hospital, now known as Yale New Haven Hospital. New Haven is known for Yale University and the World-famous Pepe's Pizza. New Haven pizza is voted #1 in the country regularly.

I was the younger of two children. My sister is three years older than me. We were a typical middle class Conservative Jewish family in many ways. We weren't very religious but I never doubted the existence of God. I went to Hebrew school. Learned to read and write Hebrew and went to synagogue twice a year for the High Holidays. Mostly to please my grandfather. I never minded doing anything to please him. I adored the man. My grandparents on my mother's side were very kind loving people. We were very close as we only lived about 12 minutes away from their home. Memories of them are sweet and warm. I hardly saw my father's family. There was some very strange dynamic in that family. We rarely saw his parents. My uncle, my father's brother lived in the house directly behind ours. They never visited each other. EVER. I suspect there were many secrets in that family. It was bizarre.

My dad went to Korea as an eighteen-year-old and when he came home Sergeant Pitkin the war hero was a different man. He NEVER spoke of the war. Come to think of it, he never spoke about anything. Nothing. He never told me anything about his parents, siblings, childhood or teenage years. He never spoke of anything beyond a surface level. He was kind and good to me. Don't misunderstand. I just wish I knew who he was. He died at 46 when I was just 18 years old. I miss him dearly.

Dad off to Korea

My mother was another story altogether. I always knew what she thought about things. She was very loud and opinionated. She was the one who introduced me to pornography. Back then

INTRODUCTION

they were called "Stag Films". They came on small 8mm reels and were obtained by someone knowing someone who handed someone else the movie in a brown paper bag. I was only 9 years old at the time. "Ma" as I used to call her would beat me for the slightest infraction. There were many beatings. This was decades before you were given a *Time Out*. It was more like, Knocked out. She would use whatever was handy. A brush, a pan, even a hammer once. Her sharpest weapon was her tongue though. Physical wounds heal but those words. We never forget them, do we?

The twelfth year of my life was when it really started to fall apart. My mother left my father for a younger lover. I'll develop that more later in the book but sufficient to say now, I felt totally abandoned. You see, she took my sister with her but didn't want me. At least that's how my 12-year-old heart saw it. About six months later I was molested by an older neighborhood boy. I changed forever after that event. I have photos of me before that event and I'm smiling and being silly. The pictures taken after show a totally different child. No smile. No expression. To this day fifty years later I can still remember how dirty and violated I felt. My innocence was stolen from me. My dad took me with him later that awful day to see the classic Clint Eastwood film, "High Plains Drifter". I have never seen that movie again. It brings back too many memories. In the parlance of our times (Yes that is a Big Lebowski reference) it's a Trigger.

Dad and I being silly

What followed is a 50-year journey of addictions, dysfunctions, depression, sex, drugs, alcohol, and a lot of loss. Loss of innocence, family and my health. I discovered God and things changed for the better when I was 25. That was the same year I got married. But what started out so beautifully took a bad turn over the next 10 years. I became a narrow-minded religious Fundamentalist. Relax there is no preaching or heavy religion in this book. I do share my spiritual journey as I discover a more balanced view of the Divine.

INTRODUCTION

But recently something wonderful happened. I finally found wholeness, peace and joy. My heart was finally healed of the wounds that started being placed there 50 years ago. This is my journey. It's a hell of a wild ride.

This is a journey of self-discovery, and Salvation. Not Salvation in the narrow Fundamentalist understanding of the word that I adopted and held for about 30 years. No not that but the way it has been properly understood since the time of Moses. Salvation means finding healing, wholeness, safety and freedom.

Let me share with you how I finally broke free. I'll give you a preview. I was willing to confront the demon that was looking back at me in the mirror. Come along and let's walk this journey together.

One word before we start. You will immediately see that most chapter titles are the titles of songs that mean a lot to me. I encourage you to listen to the music as its power to touch our hearts and change our minds is enormous. I cannot imagine a world without music. There would be no songs to sing. What a shallow existence it would be for me. Music lets our hearts feel, and minds think. It's truly a gift from above.

The Artists that most influenced me are Maurice White and Earth, Wind & Fire, The Bee Gees, Steely Dan, Billy Joel and Tears for Fears. As the Tears for Fears song "Shout" says, *Come on. I'm talking to you. Come on.*

*These are my *"Tales from the Big Chair"*. A play on the title of the Tears for Fears album *"Songs from the Big Chair"*. In 1973 there was a book called "Sybil" about a young woman with multiple personalities. The Big Chair was where she felt safe and was able to let her "selves" speak freely. So, The Big Chair

RESTORED

represents a place where one can speak freely from the heart, expressing their true self.

Chapter 1

That's Life

As mentioned earlier, I was born on September 7, 1961, at Grace New Haven Hospital, a place of historical significance, I shared a birthplace with future U.S. President George W. Bush and Karen Carpenter. New Haven, a city renowned for its rich cultural legacy, is home to the prestigious Yale University and the iconic Pepe's Pizza.

It was within the walls of our New Haven home that my love for music began to take root. Music is a part of life—at least, it has always been a part of mine. I've titled this chapter "That's Life," after the Frank Sinatra song that played often in our house when I was a kid. Growing up, our home was filled with the sounds of Sinatra, Dean Martin, and Broadway musicals.

My mother was the one who introduced me to these artists and many others. These were the voices that filled our home, their songs becoming a regular part of our everyday lives.

My father had different tastes. He shared with me the rhythms of Chicago, the sunny vibes of The Beach Boys, the laid-back tunes of the Eagles, and, most importantly, the music of the Bee Gees. The Bee Gees have been a significant part of my life, their songs sticking with me through the years. In my teenage years I was fortune enough to see the Bee Gees, Chicago with Terry Kath before he passed, and Earth, Wind & Fire with Maurice White in concert. I also saw the Beach Boys in their last concert with all the original members as Dennis Wilson would pass away shortly after the July 4th 1983 show in Atlantic City where I saw them.

Music wasn't just something in the background—it was a constant presence, shaping my memories and experiences from an early age. I still remember the first album I purchased. It was Goodbye Yellow Brick Road by Elton John.

Growing up as the younger of two children in a typical middle-class Conservative Jewish family, my early family life was rooted in tradition and community. Our household was filled with the values and customs that shaped our identity, and much of this was reinforced through our active participation in the local synagogue and Hebrew school. Attending Hebrew school was a significant part of my upbringing, where I learned not just the language but also the stories and teachings that connected me to my heritage. We were actively connected to Israel through the purchase of bonds and also tree planting projects that we contributed to. We may not have lived in Israel but Israel lives in every post holocaust Jew.

Childhood memories are everything—they shape who we are and stay with us forever. In the 1960s, childhood was defined by the freedom of the outdoors. There were no computers or iPads to keep us occupied indoors; instead, we spent our days outside, riding bikes, playing baseball, and exploring our neighborhood. It was a time when the simple joys of being active and social defined our leisure time. This era of boundless outdoor activity and face-to-face interaction made

CHAPTER 1

childhood vibrant and engaging, contrasting sharply with the more screen-oriented experiences of today's children. The thrill of those days, filled with fresh air and unstructured play, remains a cherished and nostalgic part of my early years.

My early life was deeply influenced by the loving presence of my grandparents on my mother's side, Laura and Bill. We always called them by their first names. I don't know why. Their warmth and affection provided a nurturing and stable foundation that was a cornerstone of my upbringing.

Laura and Bill were remarkable people—loving, generous, and kind. I enjoyed our many sleep overs. Bill would make me French Toast for breakfast. I try to make it exactly the same way he did, sprinkling sugar over the top. They enriched our lives by taking us on outings and ensuring we had experiences that might otherwise have been missed. My grandfather, Bill, was known for his extraordinary generosity, giving away tens of thousands of dollars to help people in need, a significant amount back in the '50s and '60s. Whether it was for medical bills, college expenses, or car repairs, he was always there to offer support.

In contrast, my father had a strained relationship with his parents and siblings, creating a disjointed family atmosphere. My uncle, who lived just behind us, and his family were practically strangers despite our close proximity. Visits between our homes were nonexistent, and interactions were minimal. My older cousins, involved in drugs during my formative years, were distant from my experiences and interests. This lack of connection on my father's side sharply contrasted with the warmth and closeness of my maternal grandparents. This divergence in familial dynamics shaped my understanding of family relationships and highlighted the profound impact of close, supportive connections versus the more complex ties of my paternal side. On one hand I desired a close family but had also learned to live in isolation from others.

Some of my favorite memories involve visiting the Bronx with my grandmother to see her father, Larry. He was a kind old man who would always give me chocolate-covered cherries and a few dollars for toys—back when $4 could buy something. Those trips to the nearby Jewish deli and dinners at Laura and Bill's home are memories I'll always cherish. Laura always brought Black and White cookies back from her trips to New York. I still love them although the ones you get in Florida are not as good as the ones from the Bronx.

My grandfather was a very successful businessman and Laura and Bill went out to eat several nights a week. We always accompanied them on Thursday nights as my father worked late that night. He owned a fine men's and women's clothing store. We went to every great restaurant in New Haven. There were so many to chose from. It was a great city with many offerings.

The smell of roasted peanuts still takes me back to the circus trips with my grandfather at the New Haven Arena. Those outings, filled with laughter and excitement, are some of the happiest moments of my childhood.

Laura and Bill's home on the Boulevard in New Haven was modest, but it was filled with valuable antiques—a testament to their passion for collecting. Yet, the most valuable thing in that house wasn't the antiques, but the love that filled every corner. Their collection grew so much that they eventually opened an antique store on Whalley Avenue. I loved tagging along with them to antique shows, soaking in the history and stories behind each piece. Those moments spent with them are memories I hold dear.

CHAPTER 1

My time in school was generally positive. I was outgoing and had a lot of friends both in the neighborhood and at school. I enjoyed activities like Little League, and these experiences were highlights of my childhood. However, this outward normalcy was often at odds with the turmoil I faced at home.

My conservative household, while nurturing in many ways, also had its challenges. The stress of my mother's frequent outbursts and abusive behavior created a dark backdrop to an otherwise vibrant childhood. At home, the constant arguments and hostility, particularly from my mother, were deeply unsettling. My father, though passive, was often caught in the crossfire, and the tension was palpable. I tried to hide from her wrath. My older sister, who is three years my senior, seemed more aligned with my mother's side, often acting more as her ally than a sibling. This dynamic added complexity to our family relationships, leaving me to deal with these emotional challenges mostly on my own.

My father was kind and good-hearted but also quiet and distant. He never spoke about his past—his childhood, his parents, or his time in the Korean War. This silence created a barrier that kept his inner world hidden, leaving me with many unanswered questions and a sense of regret for not having known him better.

The youngest of three children, my dad grew up in a conservative middle-class Jewish family of Russian immigrants, like my mother's background. My entire family migrated from Russia around the early twentieth century. We are Ashkenazi Jews. Known for his athleticism and reputation as a tough kid in high school, he joined the Marines as a teenager and commanded a tank division in Korea.

His tendency towards silence and emotional distance, which

I later inherited, shaped my own interactions with my children. I wasn't as emotionally available as I should have been. Part of it was what I learned from my father. The other part was I had suppressed a lot of my emotions. Despite these barriers, he was a devoted father. We shared many enjoyable moments, from movie outings to baseball games, and he included me in his daily activities. He hardly went anywhere without me when I was younger. That changed a bit when I became a teenager of course, but we continued to go to movies together often. His sudden death from a heart attack at 46, when I was just 18, was abrupt and unexpected, leaving a void and serving as a stark reminder of how fleeting our time with loved ones can be. I think of him everyday.

My mother came from a more privileged background. Back then young girls like her were called "Jewish American Princesses." In her youth, she was a beauty, and it was clear from the beginning that my dad was her perfect match. My mother was very young when she met my father. He was three years older than her. She was only 18 when they married in 1955. My sister came along in 1958, followed by me in 1961.

Our home on Westbrook Lane in the Westville section of New Haven was in a predominantly Jewish neighborhood. It was a place where kids could be kids. We invented games, explored the neighborhood, and made the most of our time outside. Those were the typical joys of childhood—freedom, fun, and the thrill of adventure.

But beneath the surface, my home life was overshadowed by my mother's harsh treatment. Her frequent outbursts and beatings were a constant presence in my life. I learned early on to manage her moods, always on edge, trying to avoid the wrath that could be triggered by the smallest things. The house, which

CHAPTER 1

should have been a place of safety, often felt like a battleground. I grew up with a sense of shame and embarrassment. Being molested contributed to that and it was a dark secret I held inside for decades. Also, the neighbors hearing my mother screaming was a source of deep embarrassment for me.

The dynamics between my parents were starkly contrasting and deeply troubled. My father was a quiet and reserved man, never resorting to yelling or physical punishment. Instead, he preferred to reason with me, explaining why certain behaviors were wrong, which was in sharp contrast to my mother's approach. She was loud and aggressive, frequently resorting to yelling, screaming, and hitting. This discord created a home environment filled with tension and strife, with no trace of a loving or supportive dynamic between them. I have no memories of them being affectionate or kind to each other. By the time I was twelve, their relationship had deteriorated significantly, leading to their separation. While things might have been different in the earlier years of my childhood, I don't remember any semblance of harmony between them; instead, I recall a chaotic and strained atmosphere that overshadowed any positive experiences.

My mother's abusive behavior profoundly impacted my childhood. Her physical and verbal abuse was relentless; she used whatever was at hand to punish me, from pots and pans to belts, leaving both physical and emotional scars. My parents had known each other since their teenage years, and outwardly, they appeared to be a perfect match. My grandmother even predicted that my mother would marry my father. However, beneath this facade, their relationship was fraught with problems, and my mother's abusive behavior became a dark hallmark of our family life.

When my mother left us at the age of 12 to be with a younger man, it was a devastating blow. The scandalous nature of her departure—leaving her family for someone significantly younger—caused a wave of shame and teasing from neighbors and friends. For an unmarried woman to live with a man that was not her husband in those days was very socially unacceptable. The situation was further compounded by the fact that, with no warning, my mother, along with her new partner John and my sister, packed up and left while my father was at work. I came home to find our house empty, a cruel twist that left me feeling abandoned and betrayed. I cannot imagine how my dad felt coming home to a nearly empty house. My mother never offered to include me in her new life, leaving me to deal with my confusion and hurt alone. This sense of betrayal was heightened by an unsettling encounter with an older neighborhood boy shortly after. His unwanted advances and overpowering me compounded my feelings of insecurity and fear, further isolating me at a time when I was already struggling with the upheaval in my family. I have no doubt that experience contributed to my obsession with weight lifting. I would not be overpowered again. These traumatic experiences had lasting psychological effects, influencing my attitudes toward others and shaping my interactions with men in adulthood. Even now, I remain cautious and guarded in social situations with men I don't know. These experiences deeply impacted me during those formative years. I had been propositioned many times as an adolescent by older homosexuals.

The summers I spent in California with my Uncle Sandy and his wife, Maribess, were a bright spot in my life. Those visits were a welcome escape from the turmoil at home, offering

CHAPTER 1

me a glimpse of a different world, one filled with warmth and kindness. Uncle Sandy was a kind and generous man, someone who made me feel valued and safe. He had a way of making everything seem better, even when things at home felt overwhelming.

During those summers, they took me to see television shows being filmed, like *The Bill Cosby Show, The Flip Wilson Show* and *The Carol Burnett Show*. I even got to ask Carol Burnett a question at the beginning of the show which later appeared on television. Watching these shows come to life was magical, a rare treat that filled me with excitement. For a young boy, sitting in the audience and seeing the actors perform live was an unforgettable experience. It was in these moments that I felt truly happy, as if the worries of home couldn't reach me. We also visited Universal Studios and that was a great memory. Interestingly, I have no memory of being home sad while in California. Being away from the battle zone was a welcomed reprieve.

Uncle Sandy had a deep respect for hard work, a value that had been instilled in him by my grandfather. My grandfather had started with very little, and though he became quite successful, he never forgot where he came from. He taught us that it didn't matter whether you were the waiter or the owner of the restaurant—everyone deserved the same respect. This lesson stayed with me, influencing how I viewed the world and the people around me. It was a reminder that success should never make you forget your roots or the dignity of others. The dignity and value of all human life is deeply rooted in the Jewish ethos and tradition.

Returning to New Haven, I encountered other life lessons, though they were often more challenging. I remember the scandal that erupted when an Irish Catholic family moved into our predominantly Jewish neighborhood. People in the community were not welcoming, and it was shocking to see how harshly they reacted to someone different from themselves. Later, when a bi-racial couple moved in, the reactions were even more intense. I remember some of my young friends calling their children "half breeds." Looking back, I realize that they learned such epitaphs from their parents. These experiences opened my eyes to the realities of prejudice and the struggles of acceptance. It was difficult to understand why people were treated so poorly simply because they were different. But these events also taught me the importance of tolerance and empathy. Perhaps this was all preparing me for my own bi-racial and religiously mixed family to come later? I have always judged people by how they treated and interacted with me. I never cared where they were from or what they looked like.

Interestingly, the Catholic family had two children, and one of them became a dear friend of mine, a friendship that has lasted to this day. It was a powerful reminder that despite the prejudices of others, true connections could be formed across any divide. It showed me that friendship and kindness could break through the barriers that society tried to put up. My dad and her dad were buddies as well. I have fond memories of going to their house on weekends and swimming in their pool. My dad and hers would drink beer, laugh and splash us with the waves from them doing cannonballs.

While I was learning these difficult lessons outside the home, my own family struggles continued. I witnessed the tragic outcomes of drug abuse in my cousins, Steven and Marcie. Seeing them suffer was heartbreaking, and it left a mark on me. It was a stark reminder of how easily life could spiral out

CHAPTER 1

of control and how addiction could destroy even the brightest of futures. Steven died of an overdose and Marcie ended up committing murder and dying in prison.

The neighborhood itself was not immune to tragedy. I remember the day a neighbor took his own life. The news spread quickly, and it shook everyone. For me, it was a moment that brought a deep sense of sadness and confusion. I couldn't understand how someone could feel so lost and hopeless that they would choose to end their life. It was a reality that was hard to grasp at that age, but it made me realize how important it was to pay attention to those around you and to be there for them in their darkest times.

These summers in California and the experiences in New Haven were a mix of joy and sorrow, of learning and growing. They shaped me in ways I'm still discovering, teaching me about the complexities of life, the importance of compassion, and the enduring impact of family and community. At the same time I could also be emotionally distant. I became a complex individual.

As mentioned earlier, from a very young age my mother exposed me to explicit material, a troubling experience given the stigma and secrecy surrounding such content in the 1960s, not to mention my young age. This early exposure, combined with her work at a bar with strippers, led me to witness things no child should see. Among the more unusual aspects of my childhood was this early exposure to adult themes. In the 1960s, explicit films were known as "Stag Films." They were passed around discreetly, usually acquired through a network of connections and handed off in a plain brown paper bag. Back then, pornography was neither socially acceptable nor readily available, and these films were considered taboo. It was rare for a minor to be exposed to pornography in those days. This was decades before the Internet Age. A family friend owned a restaurant where my mother worked as a bartender. On weekends they had shows featuring strippers in the downstairs lounge, and I would sneak downstairs to watch the performances. This exposure left a lasting impression on me, shaping my understanding of adult themes far earlier than most of my peers. No doubt this exposure had a lot to do with my promiscuity as I became a teenager.

Despite these challenging experiences, my childhood was not without its happy moments. The North Haven Fair was one of my favorite events, filled with rides, games, and the excitement of being part of a bustling fairground. Family vacations were another highlight, offering a break from the routine and a chance to create cherished memories. One of the most precious times was the last family trip we took together to Disneyland before my mother left us. That visit to the Magic Kingdom remains a fond memory, a snapshot of a time when our family was still together. We went as a family to California because my uncle Sandy was getting married. My grandfather purchased tickets for everyone. Pirates of the Caribbean was my favorite ride and I got a pirate tattoo at 17 to commemorate the trip and the last time we would be all together as a family.

Another sad moment came with the loss of my grandfather in 1976. He had been a pillar of strength and love throughout my childhood, offering unwavering support and affection that made the tough times more bearable. His passing marked the end of an era, leaving me with a profound sense of loss that was difficult to endure. The void left by his absence was deeply felt, and it underscored just how significant his presence had been in my life. Our family fell apart after his death. He was truly the

CHAPTER 1

Patriarch and Paterfamilias. More about him a little later.

By the time I was twelve, I had become a "Latch-Key" kid. This meant managing the house alone while my father worked. I quickly learned to cook, clean, and do laundry—skills that became essential as I navigated life without the constant presence of my parents. Music remained a crucial part of my life during this period. I discovered Blues, Soul, and R&B artists like the Dramatics, Chi-Lites, Ohio Players, and Earth, Wind & Fire. These genres became a sanctuary for me, providing comfort and a sense of escape from the difficulties I faced.

As I entered adolescence, life continued to be tumultuous. My early years, marked by family dysfunction and personal trauma, had a profound impact on who I was becoming. My mother used me as a pawn to attack my father. It's effect on me emotionally is hard to quantify. I hated being in the middle and torn. Music was my constant companion, offering solace and a reprieve from a world that often felt harsh and unforgiving.

During these formative years, I developed obsessive-compulsive disorder (OCD). Everything had to be in its proper place. I became fixated on order and symmetry. Books had to be aligned perfectly, with each one straight and even. Forks and knives had to be meticulously lined up with the plate next to them. I'm not a psychologist, but I suspect that this need for order was my way of exerting control over a life that felt chaotic and confusing. The rituals and routines I developed gave me a sense of stability and predictability, a small island of control in an otherwise turbulent world.

These early experiences and coping strategies shaped who I was during my teenage years and followed me into my adult life. Music became my safe space, and I found comfort in creating order to manage the unpredictability around me. Each day felt like a tightrope walk—trying to balance life's challenges while searching for moments of joy and stability in a world that often felt out of reach. The songs I listened to and the routines I set up helped me stay grounded and find a bit of peace amid the chaos.

Chapter 2

That's the Way of the World

Chapter Two, "That's the Way of the World," takes its name from the Earth, Wind & Fire song of the same title. The lyrics of this song resonate deeply with me: *"Child is born with a heart of gold / Way of the world makes his heart so cold."* These words perfectly capture the journey from innocence to experiencing the hardships of life. Maurice White, the visionary behind Earth, Wind & Fire, is a key figure in this story. His life and music offer powerful lessons on overcoming struggles and turning pain into something positive.

Maurice White was born in Tennessee, where he faced harsh realities like severe racism and tough living conditions. Despite these challenges, he did not let anger or bitterness define him. They say you can get better or get bitter. The choice is ours. Instead, he used music to share messages of peace, love, and healing. His songs are more than just music; they are a call for unity and a reflection of his deep spirituality.

Maurice White's story is a testament to how one can rise above difficult circumstances and use their experiences to uplift others. His ability to turn personal pain into a source of hope and inspiration make him a hero to me. His legacy shows that even in a world filled with challenges, there are people who choose to spread love and kindness, transforming their own struggles into something beautiful.

This leads us into Chapter Two, covering my early teen years. At this time, I was a young 13-year-old boy, already feeling the weight of a family torn apart by divorce and the deep pain of molestation and abandonment. My father sold our home and we moved into an apartment on Fountain Street, just a short distance from our previous home. The new street was still in the same neighborhood and conveniently close to Ernie's, my favorite pizza place. I had just finished elementary school and was about to start junior high at Sheridan Junior High, which was right down the street from our new apartment, making it easy to walk to school.

Even though the neighborhood was familiar, I was filled with fear and anxiety. I was a shy, reserved, and deeply hurt young Jewish boy, about to enter a school where most of the students were Black. This was a new and intimidating experience for me. I had heard many frightening stories about what might happen—everything from having your head flushed down the toilet, to being shoved into lockers, or beaten up. Thankfully, none of these fears came to pass. Within a few days at Sheridan Junior High, I began to feel at ease and even started to enjoy my new school.

One of the most significant moments of this period was meeting my music teacher, Mr. Carafano. He introduced me to Earth, Wind & Fire through their album *Open Our Eyes*. I still remember the first time I heard the song "Mighty Mighty." I was amazed and thought, "Who are these people?" From that moment, I became a fan of their music and connected with

CHAPTER 2

their messages. Although I was young and Jewish, I had always been a fan of Black music, especially Soul, Funk and R&B. This love for music has stayed with me throughout my life. I love to dance too. We become so attached to the artists that really speak to our hearts. Music is very unique in the effect it has on our minds and hearts. Isn't it something that you can hear a song a hundred times but you remember one time in particular. A special memory or event.

Another vivid memory from my time at Sheridan Junior High was my first crush. Her name was Judy, and she was a Black girl who was not only beautiful but also incredibly kind. I was around 13 still, in my second year at Sheridan, and Judy had completely captured my heart. I remember the final days of school that year. I was not required to attend as I had already taken and passed all my exams. But I wanted to see Judy. We didn't speak much. We would just gaze at each other and make "goo goo" eyes. Seems silly now but when you are 13 and have a crush you see it differently. During this period, the song "*My Eyes Adored You*" was playing everywhere. Its lyrics seemed to reflect my feelings perfectly: *"My eyes adored you / Though I never laid a hand on you / My eyes adored you..* The chorus, *"Carried your books from school / Playin' make believe you're married to me."* I guess that's what we were doing. Playing make believe.

It's surprising how some memories remain vivid after so many years. Judy and I came from such different backgrounds that a real relationship at that age would have been difficult. We were too young to navigate those differences. However, it's interesting that my wife is a Black woman. Ironically, Felicia, my wife, is the first and only Black woman I've ever dated; all my early girlfriends were Irish Catholic.

Reflecting on my past brings up not only personal connections but also the turbulent events of my youth. For example, in 1973, when I was twelve, our house was robbed. I wasn't at home during the robbery, but when I returned, I found that many of our antiques had been stolen. Over the years, I learned that the robbery had been staged by my mother to claim insurance money. It turned out that there had been more robberies than I realized—several other houses and businesses were targeted. My mother was involved in other schemes as well. For instance, she asked me to break the windows of her landlord's home. He owned the property where her restaurant was located. I remember a shard of glass cutting my face and lodging between my eyes, causing it to bleed heavily. A year later, after moving her restaurant to a new location, she sent me to vandalize her old restaurant. This time, I wasn't hurt, but I was seen by a business owner across the street, and my mother had to deal with the aftermath.

During my junior high years, Sunday afternoons held a special place in my heart. My grandfather would visit our apartment, and sometimes he, my dad, or the whole family would head to the Jewish deli. We'd pick up cold cuts, rye bread, and often a Bavarian cream pie for dessert, which was one of my absolute favorites. I haven't even seen it anywhere for years. More than the food, what I cherished most was spending time with my dad and grandfather. We would watch football or basketball games together depending on the season. I loved listening to their conversations and being part of those warm family moments. They often talked about my future, and my grandfather dreamed of me attending the University of Connecticut.

Everything changed in 1975. My grandfather began acting strangely. His memory was the shits, and he started saying things that were out of character and inappropriate. It became clear something was seriously wrong. After a few months of uncertainty, doctors at Yale University diagnosed him with Creutzfeld-Jakob Disease (CJD), which is the human form of Mad Cow Disease. This devastating illness rapidly destroys the brain, with an average time from diagnosis to death of about eight months. Thankfully, that's how long it took for my grandfather to pass away. It was a blessing in disguise because watching someone you love slowly deteriorate is incredibly painful. With his passing, the dream of attending UConn was lost too.

During this difficult time, I felt deep sadness for my grandmother. She was still reeling from the loss of her father, Larry. He died a few months before Bill. There was a lot of loss that year. I loved her greatly and did everything a fourteen-year-old could to comfort and help her. I took on tasks around the house, such as changing outdoor lights that required a ladder, to make things a bit easier for her. Our bond was special, and even in those tough moments, we found solace in each other. I miss both of them dearly, and their absence leaves a deep void in my heart.

As I reflect on these years, I see how they shaped who I was becoming. The challenges of moving to a new school, dealing with complex family dynamics, and experiencing the loss of loved ones all played significant roles in my development. These experiences were times of transition, filled with both pain and insight, which set the stage for the person I would become.

In addition to these personal experiences, the period from 1973 to 1976 was marked by broader social and cultural changes that influenced my world. The 1970s were a time of significant transformation in music, culture, and societal attitudes. It was the era of forced busing, affirmative action, the Sexual Revolution and Women's Lib. Earth, Wind & Fire emerged as a powerful force in this changing landscape, offering a new sound and message that resonated with many people, including myself. Their music reflected the spirit of the times, combining elements of funk, soul, and spirituality to create something truly unique and inspiring. Maurice White had provided the soundtrack of my high school years. Steely Dan and Billy Joel were also significant influences as well.

Chapter 3

Foolishness of Youth

This chapter covers my teenage years; mostly from 1975 to 1979. Growing up in the Northeast during the Golden Age of wrestling was an unforgettable experience. It was a time when wrestling was split into regional territories, each with its own unique stars and exciting stories. I remember those Saturday mornings spent glued to the TV, watching the dramatic matches of wrestlers from the Worldwide Wrestling Federation. As I reached my early teens, my love for wrestling only grew stronger.

My high school, Lee high, was in a rough part of town. Before that, I went to Sheridan Junior High in Westville, which was a good area, but the school itself wasn't great. Lee high, though, was in a bad neighborhood with a mix of different ethnic groups—lots of Italian, Black, Puerto Rican, and Asian students, and quite a few Jewish kids like me who were bused in.

Around that time, I had already started lifting weights at home when I was about 12 or 13. I developed quickly, probably thanks to some good genes from my dad. I got big and strong fast. At high school, I met an older student named Pete who was into bodybuilding. He saw my potential and invited me to work out at the YMCA. I didn't even know where the YMCA was, but Pete told me, and we agreed to meet there on a Saturday morning.

That's where I first saw Mike Katz. Mike was a famous bodybuilder from Connecticut who had won Mr. America and competed in Mr. Universe and Mr. Olympia. He was also a former football player for the Jets, but he had to quit due to a knee injury. Mike was huge—about 6' 1" and 240 pounds. When I walked into the weight room for the first time and saw him bench pressing, I couldn't believe my eyes. He had a 60-inch chest and 21-inch arms; it was like seeing a cartoon character come to life. The photo below represents what I saw that morning. From that moment on, I was hooked on bodybuilding. Mike was a big as Arnold and had a prominent role in the 1977 film Pumping Iron. The movie has become a cult classic among bodybuilders. I accompanied Mike to the New Haven premier of the film.

Mike Katz in the 70's

CHAPTER 3

Despite the excitement of those weightlifting years, I was also dealing with my own struggles. Like many teens, I was trying to figure out who I was and where I fit in. I was trying to find my place in the this world. Weightlifting offered more than just a distraction—it became a source of comfort and inspiration. It taught me about staying strong and pushing through tough times, lessons that would guide me in the future. I was very disciplined and dedicated to my bodybuilding.

Looking back, I realize that wrestling was more than just a form of entertainment. It was a way for me to understand and cope with life's ups and downs. There were good guys and bad guys. Good verses evil was always playing out on the television. The matches and the larger-than-life characters mirrored my own challenges and triumphs. Wrestling still holds a special place in my heart, reminding me of the early days when it provided both comfort and entertainment. I became friendly with some of the professional wrestlers who would train at the YMCA. Bruiser Brody and Ivan Putski were very nice to me. Putski had a son my age so we bonded quickly. Brody used to tease me a lot. I took that as his way of showing he liked me. Most people just ignore those they don't like. Bruiser Brody's real name was Frank Goodish. He was killed in Puerto Rico in 1988. His murder was never solved and those who knew him still feel as if justice was never served. Brody is a legend in wrestling around the world. I feel fortunate to have met him.

The YMCA became my daily spot after school. As I got to know everyone there. They talked with me, joked with me, but most importantly, they taught me how to lift weights properly. One guy made a big impact on me—Rich D'Angelo. Rich was about 19 when I was 14 or 15, and he treated me like a little brother. He'd pick me up, and we'd go see concerts and movies together. We went to the beach at Lighthouse Point in East Haven with the other guys from the YMCA. Rich made a lasting impression on me, and we've reconnected over the years. I've let him know how much he meant to me and how I'll never forget the kindness he showed me when I was young. Being devoted to my weightlifting and body building kept me from getting into too much trouble. I was surrounded by a lot of really good people at a time when I really needed them. I could have very easily taken a wrong turn and fallen in with the wrong crowd. Eventually I would make some poor life choices but they were not criminal.

CHAPTER 3

At Lighthouse Beach at 16

I also met other people at the YMCA who took an interest in me, like Mike Katz, and the Ugolik brothers, Joe and Stan. Joe had won Teenage Mr. America, and Stan, who was a few years older than me, won Teenage Mr. Connecticut. I'm not sure why any of these people put up with me because, as a teenager, I was a bit of a pain in the ass. But they did, and I'm grateful for that.

Mike Katz with Joe Ugolik backstage

Now Joe and I have remained friends since I was a teenager. A few years ago we were bullshitting on the phone and he casually mentions that when he was in California, while they were filming the movie Pumping Iron, that he trained arms with Arnold. I was like, Wait!, you did arms with Arnold and I'm just hearing about it now? Forty years later! If I had done

CHAPTER 3

arms with Arnold Schwarzenegger I would have had tee shirts made that said in big bold letters, **I DID ARMS WITH ARNOLD!** Joe was always an incredibly humble guy. Not me. I would have told everybody. *"Hi, I'm Randy. I did arms with Arnold."*

Arnold in the '70s

Stan's house was on my way from school to the YMCA, so I'd stop there every day. I'd sit with his mother and watch "Family Feud" while Stan got ready, and then we'd walk to the YMCA together, no matter the weather—summer, winter, rain, or snow. We didn't give a shit, we were going to work out.

During my teenage years, I made some close friends who have remained dear to me. I met John Mastroianni, Jay Barone, and Alex Trasacco when we were teenagers, and we're still friends today. Jay and John were my age and went to Notre Dame, a

Catholic high school, while Alex was a bit older and went to Hillhouse, another urban school. I went to Lee high, which was across town from Hillhouse. My parents went to Hillhouse as well. We all hung out behind Beecher School, where there was a basketball court. I used to ride my bike there, a 10–12-minute ride from my apartment. Funny enough, Beecher School was where my parents went to elementary school; my mother and dad lived just a few blocks from each other as teenagers.

Another important friend I made during that time was Kenny Appel. Kenny was a few years older than me and became a great friend. John, Kenny, and Joe were all at my wedding in 1986, and we're still good friends today. I'm thankful for that. Kenny came from a large family, and his mother was Korean, while his dad was American. They had met during the war.

Kenny, being biracial, knew what it felt like to face prejudice. He had been teased and made fun of because of his background, something that was unfortunately common back in those days. I remember one person calling Kenny "The Jap." Kenny wasn't even Japanese.

My high school years were chaotic. There were a lot of fights. By the time I was 16 or 17, I had built myself up to be very big and strong. I remember one time when a kid my age was giving me a hard time. I told him I was going to kick the shit out of him, and he ran off. Later, he came back to the schoolyard at Beecher School with his brothers, who thought they were tough guys. They rolled in on their Harley's, maybe thinking they could scare us. But at 16, me and my crew weren't afraid of anyone. We had more guts than brains.

The kid's older brother, who was in his late 20s, couldn't believe I was only 16. He said I was lying, that there was no way I could be that young because of how big I was. My friends

CHAPTER 3

backed me up, telling him, "Believe it, he's 16". In the end, there was no fight that night, and they left. But there were plenty of other fights.

I can remember getting into fights and just blacking out, not remembering anything afterward. My friends would tell me later that I was throwing people around left and right. I had this seething, burning anger inside me—a rage that I couldn't control.

But on the surface, I was a pleasant person. I've always been funny, someone who liked to smile, laugh, crack jokes, sing songs, and joke around with friends. But despite all that, I was not someone to be fucked with. And neither were most of my friends.

We started drinking at a young age too. I was about 15 when we would get beer and drink in the school yard. Harry's package store would sell to us underage kids. Sometimes we could have parties at someone's house if their parents were out. My apartment became a popular spot because my dad went out every Friday and Saturday night. To be honest, I didn't have a lot of supervision growing up. I was left alone often. There was not a lot of heart to heart talks between my dad and me. I don't fault him for his short comings. I have long realized that he was probably neglected as a child himself.

Eventually we started going to bars. There was a place downtown called Malone's that served underage kids. I started going there at 16. I remember a fight one Saturday night when we got into a brawl out front and I got arrested. It took several cops to pull me off the kid I was beating. Everyone else had the sense to run away when they heard sirens, but I was in a blackout rage. We were mischievous kids. I remember one time we rolled a car on its side across the street from the school. We didn't get caught that time. The shenanigans we pulled were endless back then.

There a few other stories during my time at the YMCA that I want to share with you. The best part about being there was the camaraderie. As I mentioned earlier, we would go to the beach together, the movies (including the time they snuck me into my first X-rated film), grab meals, and attend bodybuilding contests. We did a lot together and shared so many laughs.

One story I'll never forget is the time Ron was doing chin-ups, and he thought it would be funny to pull his pants down as a joke. He didn't just pull down his pants—he pulled down his underwear too. So there Ron was, doing chin-ups with his balls swinging around like walnuts in the wind. It was hilarious. But don't try that at a gym like Planet Fitness today; I don't think you can get away with things like that anymore.

In the summer of 1976, I was still 14 and competed in my first bodybuilding contest. I was the youngest competitor there and even got interviewed by WNBC News Channel 4 from New York. That was a big deal for me. I loved going to the shows. Each year, guest posers from California would come because Mike Katz, who was the promoter, would bring them in. Mike knew everybody in the business and he would train with Arnold at Gold's Gym in Venice California during the summers. The greats from the Seventies were there—Robby Robinson, Ed Corney, Boyer Coe. I remember one show in Waterbury where I competed, and Frank Zane was the guest poser. I still have the program from that show around here somewhere and my name is in it.

My mother had a restaurant in a strip mall on Whalley Avenue, one of the main streets in New Haven. The place next door was like a bodega—a small shop where you could grab coffee, soda,

CHAPTER 3

cigarettes, and other stuff. A teenager who worked there started mouthing off to my mother, swearing and giving her a hard time. When my mother told me about it, that was all I needed to hear.

I called up my friends John and Jay, who always had my back. Now that I think of it, whenever we needed each other there was never an explanation given, it was just "get in the car". We walked into the store, and without a word, I calmly went behind the counter, grabbed the kid by his neck, lifted him off the ground, and slammed him onto the floor. I smashed his head against the floor a few times and told him, "Don't you ever speak that way to my mother again. If I have to come back here, I'll really hurt you. Do you understand what I'm saying to you?" The kid was terrified, begging for mercy, saying, "Yes, sir. Yes, sir, please. I'm sorry, sir".

As he lay there, he mentioned something that puzzled me. He said, "They've already been here. They've already been here to talk to me". I had no idea what he was talking about, so I wrapped things up and went next door to give my mother the report. When I told her what happened, she revealed that a couple of guys in a Lincoln Continental had already gone into the store to have a "talk" with the kid. My mother had "friends"—friends who had already paid the young man a visit and scared the shit out of him.

When I walked back to her restaurant there were about a dozen cops there eating. She always had a lot of cops there. They congratulated me for standing up for my mother and taking care of business. Family honor was important to us and the cops had no misgivings about my behavior. Things were very different back then. I knew a lot of cops and even thought about becoming one myself for a while. Several were very close family friends that would come to the house for dinner on the holidays.

These violent outbursts were not isolated. Another notable incident occurred when I was leaving my mother's restaurant. A Black man parked behind my car, blocking me in. He had just come out of Kentucky Fried Chicken with his date. I approached his window and politely asked him to move his car so I could get out. He responded with a cocky attitude, saying, "Make me." So, I did. I reached into his car, grabbed him by the neck, and dragged him out. I started punching him because he refused to move his car. Where my mother's restaurant was located there was a lot of racial tension and decisions were quickly made how you would react to someone based on their appearance. Apparently this gentleman decided because I was White that he would not move his car. He made a poor decision. It was infuriating that he chose to act tough rather than simply move his vehicle. Asshole.

John and I had a funny experience one night driving home from his girlfriend's home. A car pulled up behind us with four large Black guys. There were a lot of racial tensions in the city at that time and we didn't know their intentions. John always thought everyone wanted to fight him. So because we were outnumbered John says, *"Look big!"* *"What the fuck does that mean?"* I asked him. He wanted me to sit up in my seat as if I were standing up to seem larger and taller. He did the same. The car behind us pulled off and turned down a side street. I have no idea if our *looking big* deterred them but we have laughed about that episode for over forty years.

But it wasn't all drama. There were plenty of good times too, especially the concerts. I remember seeing Earth, Wind & Fire, Boston, and even going with my dad to see the Bee Gees. I got to see Chicago with Terry Kath before he passed away. I must have seen Earth, Wind & Fire about six times during the '70s when they came to New Haven. The first time I went, I was 14, and I felt like I was the only white person in the crowd. I still remember the smell of reefer in the air. But over the years, the crowd became more and more integrated, reflecting the universal appeal of Earth, Wind & Fire's music. Their music was all about pride in who you are without malice towards others, and it brought people together.

Then came the girlfriends. There were a lot of those over the years. Jackie was the first girl who showed an interest in me. She was an Irish Catholic girl who lived near Beecher School. I was incredibly shy back then and had no clue how to make a move or talk to a girl. In those days, if a girl liked a guy, she'd tell her girlfriend, who would then pass on the message. Sometimes, she'd even suggest asking the girl to go ice skating—a favorite hangout of mine. Those were simpler times, but they were etched into my memory in their own special way.

At Edgewood Park, there was an ice-skating rink where we spent most of our winters. We loved it. The smell of the fire, drinking hot chocolate, sitting next to the warmth, and skating with the fresh, cool air in our faces—it was invigorating, and I truly loved it. I wasn't the best skater, but I enjoyed it anyway.

That winter, I gathered the courage to talk to Jackie, and she eventually became my first girlfriend. We were innocent back then—just a little kissing. What stands out the most is that, at just 14, I bought her a tiny diamond ring from a jewelry store. I did this because, despite my family being broken, I longed for a family of my own. I wanted to love and be loved. I was very young and broken. There was an emptiness inside I was trying to fill. Jackie and I didn't last long, maybe a few months, but I remember the fun times we had—going to the park, ice skating, flying kites, and taking walks. It was a simpler, more innocent time compared to today.

Then there was another girl, whom I'll refer to as "E" to keep her identity private. I met her at Beecher School, where we often hung out at the basketball court behind the school. One evening, a girl from our group approached me with a knowing smile and said, "E likes you and wants to go out with you." She paused, then added, "In fact, she's looking for more than that."

I was taken aback and a bit intimidated. While I understood what she was hinting at, I had no idea how to handle it. The prospect both fascinated and terrified me, leaving me feeling a mix of excitement and uncertainty. As a 15 year old buying condoms was a terrifying experience. I felt like everyone was watching me and going to tell my father.

E and I ended up going out for some time. We were both 15 at the time. She was a sweet girl, but she had a troubled home life. Her dad was a well-known and respected doctor in New Haven, but her mother was an alcoholic. I can still remember calling her after school, and her mother would answer the phone, completely shitfaced. Despite her own struggles, E became my first. She was the first girl I had that kind of relationship with.

The summer before my senior year of high school, my life took a big turn when my dad remarried. It was a tough adjustment. My new stepmother and I didn't get along. She had a way of making me feel like I didn't belong in my own home. It felt like she was trying to push me out, making room for herself and my father. My dad kept reassuring me with his usual line, "She knows you come first," but I had my doubts about how true that was. Living with her was a struggle, and I didn't like it.

We had moved from our old place on Fountain Street to a

CHAPTER 3

condo in Branford after my father remarried, which was a much nicer area. But this change brought another challenge. Since Branford was its own school district, I needed a car to get to school—there was no school bus for kids like me from New Haven going to Lee High School. So, as soon as I turned 16, my dad took on the daunting task of teaching me how to drive. My initial attempts were so nerve-wracking that I nearly gave him a heart attack. He was a bundle of nerves, and I couldn't blame him. He was a smoker and he was really puffin those things during my driving lessons. Eventually, I managed to get the hang of it, and after all the close calls and shaky moments, we both made it through in one piece. After E there was another Irish Catholic girl named Nancy. The only remarkable thing about that relationship was the I met her and her friend Shirley when I was hanging out with Al Trasacco. He ended up going out with Shirley and I went out with Nancy. I remember sitting at the kitchen table talking to Nancy's mother when we got the news that Elvis had died. Some things you never forget.

The following year I found myself in a steady relationship with a girl named Joanne. I'd first met her at a New Year's Eve party the year before. Although I can't quite remember if she was dating anyone at that time, she made an impression on me. Joanne was charming, Irish Catholic and her affluent family lived in Orange, a town known for its wealthier residents. I used to really enjoy the scenery riding my motorcycle to her house.

Joanne was my first real love. It was that intense, all-consuming teenage love. Joanne had a wild side. She had an insatiable desire for intimacy, wanting to be physical almost every day. As a 16- and then 17-year-old, this was an intense relationship and I was in over my head.

The first time I spent the night with her was when her parents were away. I told my father I was staying with friends. It reminds me of the song "O What a Night" by Frankie Valli. This was the first time I spent the night with a girl. The next day, I felt a strange mix of pride and adulthood as I bought us a six-pack of St. Pauli Girl beer. I felt grown up but I was growing up too fast.

What I didn't realize until later was that Joanne's grandmother, who was supposed to stay in her own part of the house, had seen me in Joanne's room. Joanne had to handle the awkward fallout with her grandmother, but as far as I know, her mother never found out. It's funny, E, Jackie, Nancy and Joanne were all Irish Catholic. Later in the story is another Irish Catholic girl Kathy, who is even more significant. New England is made up of many ethnic communities. Irish, Italian, Greek, Jewish, Polish and others. I guess where I grew up had more Irish Catholic girls to choose from. Oddly enough, I never had a Jewish girlfriend.

During this time, I decided to move out of my father's condo and return to live with my mother. It wasn't a decision I was particularly proud of, but it was one felt I had to make considering the friction with my stepmother.

John, my mother's partner, had left her. He wanted children, but after her hysterectomy, that wasn't possible. They decided to part ways, and he moved out of state. With him gone, my mother, who had left me to live with my dad for five years, asked me to come live with her. I was hesitant at first because of how she had treated me when I was younger. But my mother knew exactly how to play on my feelings. She used my dislike for my stepmother to drive a wedge between me and my dad.

The part that hurt the most was that I ended up leaving my father in the same way my mother had left him. While he was at work, I went to the condo with a few of my mother's friends—men I knew from before. We packed up my bed, dresser, and stereo equipment and moved everything out.

Looking back, I'm sure my father felt the same heartbreak and loss he had experienced years before. My stepmother told me he was devastated. Even though the decision to move was really my mother's, I still have heavy regret about how it all played out. My father and I didn't speak for months after that. We would reconcile soon however.

On my motorcycle at 17

So, during my senior year, I moved in with my mother. While she was at work every day, the house was ours, and Joanne and I spent a lot of time together. About nine months into our relationship, Joanne became pregnant. Her mother took her to an abortion clinic, and they ended the pregnancy. I was deeply upset, but it was done without my input, and I found out only after the fact. The strain of this event was too much for our relationship, and it ended soon after. There was a popular song at that time called *"Fool (If You Think It's Over)"* by Chris Rea. It's about feeling like it's all over after a great love loss. That song resonated with me at that time. It's funny how songs stay with you and become the soundtrack of your life. "Maybe I'm a Fool" by Eddie Money was another song from those years. He sings about still loving one who has moved on from you. For a time I was still hanging on like a fool.

As I moved on from those tough years, I hit another big milestone. My high school graduation in June 1979 was a major event. It took place at historic and beautiful Woolsey Hall, right on the campus of Yale University. The setting was grand and impressive, a place with so much history, and it felt like a fitting place to mark the end of that chapter of my life. Walking across that stage in Woolsey Hall was a proud moment. All the hard work, the ups and downs, the challenges—it all led up to that day. Seeing my friends and classmates there, knowing we had all made it, was a great feeling. The atmosphere was filled with excitement and a bit of nervous energy, as we were all stepping into the next phase of our lives. The theme of the graduation was *"Ain't no Stoppin' us Now,"* after the McFadden and Whitehead song that was very popular at the time. Graduating in such a historic venue made the day even more memorable, and it's something I'll always look back on with pride.

By September, just after my 18th birthday, I moved out from my mother's for good and never returned. This new beginning was a chance to leave behind the challenges of those years and start over.

Chapter 4

Movin out

"Movin Out" covers the years from 1979 to 1985, my adult life prior to marriage. I have always liked the song "Movin Out" by Billy Joel, and now I find myself in the process of moving out. During the summer of 1979, I frequently visited a nightclub located on Whitney Avenue in downtown New Haven, known as Studio 71. The love of disco music and dancing drew me to this venue. That summer, my friend Mike Pantera experienced some discord with his parents. Mike was a friend I met at the YMCA. He was about four years older than myself. Consequently, Mike spent about a week staying with me at my mother's. Upon my turning 18, Mike and I decided to rent an apartment in the Fair Haven area of New Haven on Pine Street. The residence was an older two-family home, typical of New England, likely around 70 to 80 years old. Our apartment was situated on the upper floor and was completely unfurnished, containing only our beds and dressers. I recall having a clock radio in the kitchen, which provided us with music. I have memories of hearing the song "Lovin, Touchin, Squeezin" by Journey coming out of that little radio. As I mentioned earlier, you can hear a song a hundred

CHAPTER 4

times but there is always that one time that stands out in your memory. Mike and I used to play pranks on each other. There was no light in the stairway going up to our apartment. One night I hung a scary Halloween mask from the door frame and when he turned the light on to enter the apartment, he screamed when he saw it. I got a good laugh out of that. I knew pay back was coming though.

Both Mike and I secured jobs as bouncers at Studio 71, where my friend Joe also worked. After approximately a year, both Joe and Mike chose to leave their positions at Studio 71, as they no longer wished to continue in that role. By this time, I had become deeply immersed in the nightlife and opted to stay. Later, around 1980, we moved to another apartment on Young Street in the Westville area of New Haven. This new residence was also a multi-family dwelling, and Mike, Joe, and I shared the second floor. Our living arrangement was pleasant, and we all got along well, although I admit I could be quite difficult at times. During this period, my drinking and cocaine use escalated as I became increasingly integrated into the disco scene. I vividly remember attending many parties at the home of a man named Ernie, a well-known restaurateur in New Haven who owned one of the city's most prestigious upscale restaurants. He would often visit our club, entering the DJ booth once I began my career as a DJ, and would casually produce a cocaine spoon.

After approximately a year and a half of working as a bouncer and subsequently as a doorman, I transitioned into the role of a DJ, driven by my passion for music. This led me to immerse myself deeper into the disco scene, where I indulged in cocaine, increased my alcohol consumption, and engaged with many women. Our gatherings often took place after hours at Ernie's, a beautiful home located off Whitney Avenue in a pleasant area of New Haven.

One memorable incident occurred at Ernie's restaurant, where I was enjoying drinks with friends. While retrieving my coat from the coat room, Ernie followed me, placed his foot on mine to prevent me from moving, and attempted to kiss me. I instinctively pushed him away, asserting that I was not interested. He quickly apologized, explaining that he found me attractive. I expressed my gratitude for the compliment but requested that such advances not occur again, and he respected my wishes. Ernie, a Gay man, passed away several years after our acquaintance due to AIDS, a disease that devastated the Gay community during the 1980s.

I relished the nightlife, enjoying drinking, cocaine, and the company of women. During this period, I made trips to New York City, including a visit to Studio 54 with another friend also named Mike, who was the previous DJ at Studio 71. We spent all our money and found ourselves in need of cash for the tolls on our return ride home, prompting me to approach a hooker for assistance. My charm with women proved effective once again, as she provided me with some money and even gifted me an unused condom as a keepsake. It was indeed a memorable night. I frequently ventured into the city with friends to go to bars, occasionally visiting the sex shops that were prevalent in Times Square. New York City was a gritty and chaotic place during the late 1970s and early 1980s, and I had witnessed a great deal. However, I was never inclined towards live sex shows or strip clubs; if physical interaction was not possible, I saw little value in the experience. When I would go to Gindee's, the only strip club in town at the time, I would play Pac-Man. I had no interest in "making it rain." I went because I wanted to be

CHAPTER 4

with my friends.

In the early 1980s, specifically around 1980-81, a group began frequenting Studio 71, which we referred to affectionately as the Transit Authority. This group consisted of three transvestites who also worked as prostitutes in New Haven. They were Black and one of them was named Minnie. Although I never learned Minnie's real name, she once mentioned that we attended high school together. However, Minnie never disclosed her true identity. I cannot recall the name of the second individual, but the third, whom I remember distinctly, was named Clarence, with the female name of Kenisha. Clarence and I developed a friendship, often spending time together at nightclubs and house parties. He was seldom in drag when we hung out. This was prior to my religious indoctrination, and I was indifferent to others' sexual orientations, as long as they understood my own. A memorable incident occurred one evening when I was driving Kenisha home. She bore a striking resemblance to Donna Summer, being exceptionally attractive. As I was about to say goodnight, Kenisha leaned over to kiss me. However, I quickly realized the situation and pulled back, laughing as I questioned her actions. She joined in the laughter, and that was the end of that encounter. This was one of the few times Clarence was in drag when we went out. I would joke on occasion that "you almost got me."

In the summer of 1980, I traveled to California with my friend Mike Pantera. Our itinerary included Los Angeles, Venice Beach, and Gold's Gym, which we thoroughly enjoyed. After renting a car, we drove along the Pacific Coast Highway, making our first stop in San Francisco. We had a wonderful time visiting Fisherman's Wharf, Pier 39 and navigating Lombard Street. Following our stay in San Francisco, we continued our journey to my uncle's home in Sacramento, where he was still married to Maribess, and his sons, Mark and David, were young boys at that time. Our visit there was quite enjoyable.

Mike was a very likable, well mannered guy and Sandy's family were happy to host us. I was always well mannered around my friends' parents, and they all thought I was a sweet kid. I was raised to be respectful of my elders. We were all like that. I always enjoyed visiting with my friends' parents. They made me feel like a part of the family and I really loved how that made me feel.

After approximately a week, Mike returned home to Connecticut. I, on the other hand, was reluctant to leave; I had grown fond of my surroundings. My uncle, aunt, and cousins represented the only semblance of a normal family I had ever encountered in my family, and I cherished my time there. California appealed to me greatly, and I wished to remain. My memories of California from my earlier years left an indelibly good impression on me. My uncle, a gastroenterologist employed at Kaiser Permanente, suggested that I stay with them. He offered to assist me in finding a job at the hospital and enrolling in college. This proposal seemed like a promising opportunity for me to establish a stable and fulfilling life. I was determined not to return to Connecticut, as I sought to distance myself from my mother and the chaos that accompanied my past. I reached out to my father, expressing my desire to stay and requesting his assistance in acquiring a car. However, he declined, insisting that I return home. In hindsight, during a conversation with my wife, she suggested that perhaps my father believed he could provide for me just as well as my uncle could. While I had not considered this perspective before. I was unwilling to return to New Haven, a place filled with painful

CHAPTER 4

memories and negative experiences. In contrast, California was a source of peace and positive recollections.

Ultimately, I returned home after about a week, harboring resentment towards my father and unwilling to communicate with him. A few weeks later, my father suffered a sudden heart attack and passed away unexpectedly. At that time, I was employed at my mother's restaurant, as she owned and operated bars and restaurants. When the phone rang, my stepmother informed my mother of the tragic news, and my mother said matter-of-factly "Daddy's dead." I got on the phone and spoke to my stepmother. She told me what happened. I started crying and couldn't speak. I gave the phone back to my mother. I was devastated. I loved my father. It just happened to be a moment of anger, and I was a very angry young man. I know that in time I would have reconciled with him as I had in the past.

The guilt of never getting to say goodbye and of knowing that he died while we were fighting, haunted me for decades. I finally worked through it, and I don't have the guilt anymore. He died on July 23rd, 1980. So in 1976 my grandfather and great grandfather would pass away. Then my dad in 1980. The following year 1981, my step mother would be killed in a car accident. I wasn't close to her but it was another loss.

While working at the club at night, I was working for my mother during the day. She had a young woman named Kathy working for her as a waitress. Kathy was four years my senior and was attending Southern Connecticut State College, where she was pursuing a degree in Special Education. Kathy developed an affection for me and actively sought my attention. She was an attractive, petite young woman, also Irish Catholic. What else? As our relationship progressed and became serious, we dated for a year and a half, during which I became engaged to her. We traveled to New Hampshire for me to meet her parents. She hailed from Enfield, Connecticut originally, located approximately an hour from New Haven. I had the opportunity to meet her family members both in Enfield and in New Hampshire, and I found her parents and the rest of her family to be really nice people. The salt of the earth. Kathy had three sisters and one brother, contributing to a lovely family dynamic. I was as desirous of being part of her family as I was about being with her.

Throughout my courtship with Kathy, I explored various educational institutions in an effort to establish a stable future for us. I began an apprenticeship in printing, where I learned both offset and web printing techniques. Subsequently, I enrolled in a computer school located about a 30 to 40-minute drive from New Haven, in Bridgeport. At that time, I was residing in Hamden with my friends Kenny and Joe, and my daily commute to school involved walking a mile to the bus stop, taking one bus downtown, transferring to another bus to reach the train station, and finally taking a train from New Haven to Bridgeport. This routine was repeated five times a week for what was to be a nine-month program. However, about six months in, I grew weary of the constant travel. I struggled as a young man to envision my future and failed to grasp the importance of planning; I did not understand that failing to plan equates to planning to fail. This lesson eluded me in my youth, as I could not see beyond the immediate moment. Remember the quote in the opening of the book. *People raised in love see things differently than those raised in fear.*

Subsequently, I opted to enroll in a different educational institution, one that was local and situated on the Boulevard,

CHAPTER 4

approximately two miles from my grandmother's residence. This was the Connecticut School of Electronics, and I made the decision to attend. Midway through the program, I became disillusioned and chose to pursue a career as a full-time disc jockey, which I found to be enjoyable and financially rewarding. Kathy would accompany me to the club, and during that period, I was not involved with other women or substance abuse, although we did indulge in moderate drinking. Kathy eventually moved to Enfield, an hour away from New Haven, after securing a teaching position. For a period she was renting my old room at my mother's house. She lived with her aunt and uncle, who were a kind and welcoming family. Eventually she moved into her own apartment, and I would spend weekends with her in Enfield. Other times she would spend the weekend with me in Hamden.

Unfortunately, the distance became a significant barrier. While in Enfield, Kathy met a young businessman, and it seemed she believed her prospects were brighter with him than with me. In hindsight, I acknowledge that she may have been correct. However, her decision to end our relationship left me heartbroken. The thing that was the worst of it was we slept together all weekend and as I am about to leave to go back home, she says she wants to end our engagement. What kind of woman spends the weekend sleeping with a man knowing she wants to break up? I had deep feelings for her and envisioned a future together, even converting to Catholicism for her.

I vividly recall a conversation with my mother at her restaurant, where she expressed her disapproval of my lifestyle choices concerning Kathy. In that moment, I couldn't help but reflect on her own decisions, particularly her departure from my father when I was just twelve years old. So, you decided to shack up with a younger guy, but when he left you because you couldn't have kids, you ended up with a married New Haven cop who had kids of his own; I think to myself. Not exactly the example of virtue to be lecturing me. The tension with my mother was thick, and I could feel the anger just waiting to burst. It wouldn't be much longer until I would finally leave New Haven and her influence.

Now that Kathy's gone, I'm back in the nightlife scene, hanging out with my DJ friends at clubs, trying to meet girls, and getting deeper into cocaine and drinking. One of my buddies, Willie, was the DJ at Daniel's, which was the biggest club in New Haven for a while. It opened in the winter of '80 and was really nice, with several bars, a big dance floor, plus a killer sound system. There was also a smaller downstairs area where the music was softer, making it easier to chat.

I remember one girl I met there. Her name was Maureen. She was an ex-girlfriend of one of my buddies. She was adorable, sweet and you guess it, Irish Catholic. I really liked her. She came home with me and spent the night, but we didn't have sex. I had done that with several women. This may sound terrible but it seemed that I didn't sleep with the girls I really liked. I remember going to the St Patty's Day parade with her soon after we started seeing each other. I can remember her reaching out to hold my hand and me trying to shake her hand instead. I was a smooth talker and had a way with the ladies but even I didn't have a perfect record. It was a comical moment. Mr Cool could be a goof at times. We dated for a while, and it was a nice relationship. There was not a lot of drama until I met her sister. I tried to pull off the impossible. The double dip. Yes, I tried to date her sister behind her back. Back then I almost felt compelled to date every girl I could. It was like I was trying to

CHAPTER 4

prove something. I don't know if it was because I was molested that I was trying to prove how masculine I was or because I had such poor relationships with the female figures in my life that I was compensating somehow. I don't know. All I know is the double dip among sisters is not possible. So, while trying to double down I lost both of them. It was a stupid thing to do and made no sense because I really liked Maureen.

I have done a lot of things that made no sense over the years. I didn't mourn for long. I was back at the club seducing another girl the next night. I was a decent looking young man and well-built, but I wasn't Brad Pitt. But I had a way with the girls and knew they liked me. Maybe it was my confidence they were attracted to? All I know is that I had more girls than any of my friends. Later in the story when I moved to Atlantic City, I would continue my womanizing ways. I've had dozens and dozens of girlfriends. I say that not to brag but to highlight that I was desperately trying to fill a void inside.

Getting back to Daniel's. I knew all the bouncers from the gym, so I never had to wait in line or pay a cover charge. It felt pretty awesome, honestly. Don Muraco was a professional wrestler for the WWF at the time and a friend from the gym. He was the Intercontinental Champion at the time and here I was partying with him at Daniel's. Willie was the DJ there, and he was super well-known in Connecticut for being one of the best. Since I was now DJing at Studio 71, we hit it off and started hanging out, chatting about music, and indulging in coke together. Before I knew it, I was diving deeper into that lifestyle, going to parties with him. At 19, I was spiraling out of control. My mother decided to close the restaurant where I met Kathy and opened a bar next door called Gag's on Whalley Ave in New Haven. It was run by two Italian brothers, the Gagliardi's, and was famous for stag parties, which are basically bachelor parties. My mother bought the bar from them. They had strippers and hookers, making it quite the classy establishment. My mother revamped the place a bit, but the stag parties and hookers were still a thing. There were even beds downstairs for the guys to take the hookers. My mother got a cut from all that. My mother's place was a brothel.

Then there was this girl, a teenager named Teri, who was a couple of years younger than me. I had seen her a few times at my mother's place, but I never really paid her much attention. One night, she came looking for me, but I wasn't around, so she asked my mother where I was. For some reason, my mother told her about the club I used to hang out at. Teri ended up coming down to find me. I was pretty drunk and high, as usual, and we hit it off. She came back to my place with me, and that's how we became a couple. This was during my wild Times Square days with friends, hitting up sex shops and bars, just living it up. But then I started to settle down a bit. I don't want to sound like I had a Messiah complex or anything, but I saw something innocent in her despite her being a prostitute. While she was with me, she was not in that occupation anymore. She had a rough past, having been abused by her father, and I felt a lot of compassion for her. So, she moved in with me for a while. I did everything I could to help her establish a normal life for herself.

Now, about the porn industry—having seen a lot of it, especially when I was younger, I really dislike how it shapes young people's views on sex. They think what they see in those films is how they should act, but it's just raw sex and lacks any real connection. We now know from science that pornography has deleterious effects on a young developing mind. To think that a young man can view images of women being exploited and not attain sexist or worse abusive attitudes toward women is ridiculous. I was not immune to this poison. As I grew older, it all started to feel vulgar to me. Many women in the industry are trafficked and that makes it all the more repulsive to me.

As much smut as I was witness to, I also gleaned from movies and television the idea of making love. An intimate relationship with warmth, tenderness, hugging, and kissing. Sadly, I have participated in both. In the Sixties and Seventies pornography was available but it was not as easy to attain as it is today. Most teenagers had not seen porn in those days. Today kids as young as seven or eight are viewing it online. The Internet has turned into a real cesspool. With a cellphone, anyone can access videos of anything you can think of. I am a Libertarian when it comes to adults. But I am passionate about protecting children from adult themes. Whether I agree morally or not about certain issues, I believe adults should have the freedom to make their own choices. The obvious caveat is that they are not causing harm to anyone. I learned long ago that my religious views should not be imposed on others. The country is not a big church.

Chapter 5

Atlantic City

Now, back to Willie. Willie loved heading to Atlantic City to gamble, and a few times he asked me, "Hey, want to join me for a trip to Atlantic City after the club closes?" I was like, "Sure, I'm in!" Now, Willie had this tiny two-seater sports car—can't remember the exact model, maybe a TR7 or something similar. Anyway, since he had a girlfriend, she ended up sitting on my lap during our rides to Atlantic City. It was a three-and-a-half-hour drive, so by the time we arrived, my legs were totally numb. We made that trip probably three times. I remember one weekend we stayed over, but I lost all my cash within the first hour, which was typical for me. While wandering the boardwalk, I started noticing these folks involved in the timeshare business. I didn't even know what that was back then. I chatted with some young people my age who were handing out coupons to tourists, inviting them to check out a souvenir shop for a pitch about attending a timeshare presentation. If you sat through the presentation, you'd get a gift—a dice clock, which was basically a clock with dice for numbers. For some reason, back in '81 and '82, people

CHAPTER 5

thought that was the coolest thing ever and really wanted one.

They went to these presentations, and outside on the boardwalk, there was someone handing out coupons, known as a runner. Inside the store, the person was called an OPC, which I learned stands for outdoor public contact. I asked the guys how to land a job like that, and they told me to head to the office and chat with the owner, Richard. He was a young guy whose dad had started the business and was big in Las Vegas. Richard decided to set up shop in Atlantic City on the boardwalk. They offered me a job as a runner right away and asked when I could start. I said I could be there in a couple of days. So, I went back to New Haven and told Kenny and Joe I was off to Atlantic City. Teri went to her mother's house. I took a bus with my suitcase and arrived in AC. My first place wasn't really an apartment; it was a room I rented on Pacific avenue near California avenue. It was an old rooming house with at least three or four floors. One thing stands out in my memory of that summer. The song "Planet Rock" was playing everywhere. All day long that's all I heard. We didn't have air conditioning so with the windows open, "Rock Rock to the Planet Rock" was all I heard around the clock. These were the days when everyone was walking around with a huge Boom Box.

Apparently, rooming houses used to be super popular in Atlantic City because folks from Pennsylvania and other parts of New Jersey would come to vacation for the summer or just spend weekends. After a couple of weeks, I managed to find a two-room apartment in Ventnor, which is just down the road from Atlantic City. If you're not familiar, it's an island with Atlantic City, Ventnor, Margate, and then Longport at the end, where all the wealthy folks live. It's an upscale area, like Westport or Greenwich in Connecticut. Anyway, I moved into this two-room apartment on South Victoria avenue in Ventnor, right by the beach.

I could crack open my windows and listen to the ocean. I really loved the sound and smell of it. Eventually I head back to Connecticut since all my stuff is at my grandmother's place in the attic. I had my dresser, my clothes, my stereo, and my album collection up there. Willie helps me out, and we haul everything back to Ventnor, where I get comfy in my little two-room apartment. He borrowed a station wagon for the move. I call Teri and say, "Hey, you can come down now! I've got a spot for us". She makes her way over, and as my grandmother used to say, we went into housekeeping. This was back in 1982, and I was 20, living near Atlantic City with my girlfriend.

That summer, I was working on the boardwalk, but soon I felt so weak I could barely stand. I told Richard, "I don't know what's up with me, man. I feel really sick". He looked at me and said, "You know, the way you're describing it sounds a lot like what my brother had—hepatitis B. Maybe that's what's going on with you." Richard was a good guy and gave me the name of his family doctor. I went to see Dr. Michael Sloteroff, who was super nice. It was a Jewish family practice with Dr. Michael, his brother, and their dad all working together. Dr. Michael took one look at me and said, "Get this guy in quarantine right away." He could tell I had hepatitis just by looking at me; my eyes were as yellow as potato chips! After some blood work, it turned out my liver function levels were off the charts. So there I was, stuck at home trying to recover from hepatitis B. Back then, there weren't many treatments available—just had to tough it out until you felt better. It took me many months to recover from that illness. I didn't have much cash, but thankfully my grandmother helped me out since she knew I was too sick to

CHAPTER 5

work. She sent me about $500 a month, which wasn't a fortune, but it helped.

I think our rent was around 275 bucks. It wasn't much, which left us a bit of cash for food, and Teri had picked up a part-time job. After about a year and a half with her, I'd had enough. Teri was struggling with alcoholism, likely due to all the trauma and abuse she faced in her early life, including her time as a teenager on the streets. She used alcohol to cope. Her drink of choice was Hennessy, a cognac, and let me tell you, when she drank, she transformed into a totally different person—like a monster. I can't count how many times I'd get calls from her while she was down in Atlantic City, I'd have to drop everything to go get her. Or I'd be at our apartment in Ventnor, trying to manage her drunken escapades. One night, she was particularly out of control and just snapped, hitting me. I remember lying on the bed when she kicked me under the chin, breaking a tooth. I finally snapped and told her to get out. I packed her stuff in a bag and tossed it on the sidewalk, saying I was done. I can be a procrastinator, but once I make up my mind, that's it.

A little bit of trivia for you. In the Monopoly game, all the streets are named for streets in Atlantic City, Ventnor and Margate.

Fast forward to 1983, I moved to Margate, which is a really nice, mostly Jewish area that I loved. I rented a room in another boarding house and spent that summer partying, drinking, and meeting new girls. Eventually, I got tired of the boardwalk scene and decided to take a job at a local grocery store, a family-owned place that was run by a Jewish family called Casel's.

They hired me right away since I had some kitchen experience from my mother's restaurants. I started working in the deli, and there was this older guy named Eddie who showed me the ropes.

He taught me how to cut meat properly and even how to make roast beef, corned beef, and coleslaw. We made everything from scratch, and let me tell you, it was all top-notch and super delicious. I really enjoyed my time there. I worked at Casel's from 1983 to 1984 on and off, and it was a nice change from the boardwalk scene. I met Rodney Dangerfield while working there. He was performing at Resorts Casino and staying at a home in the area. He ordered a Corned Beef Special which I promptly made. He was wearing a bath robe at two in the afternoon. We chatted for a few minutes and he was pleasant.

Then, during the summer of '83, I met this girl named Beth. I was 22, working at the deli, and she was a teenager but super cute and smart. We hit it off, and I had no clue about her age when I asked her out to a movie. She said yes and gave me her number. That Friday night we saw "The Natural" with Robert Redford. Beth was from Boyertown Pennsylvania and was in Margate for the summer babysitting for a wealthy family. She had a lot of free time, so we went on walks, grabbed ice cream, and went to the movies together. My favorite part was when I joined Casel's softball team. I loved playing, and she would come to watch me. I was a solid hitter, even if I was slow as shit. I remember one game where I hit four home runs! The opposing team didn't know what hit them. I had a buddy named Tony back then who would come to the games and sit in the stands holding a "John 3:16" sign. If you know, you know.

But honestly, that summer was a blast, and what I loved most about it—and about Beth—was how innocent our relationship was. There was no hooking up or anything like that; we were just like a regular boyfriend and girlfriend, which is how it should've been when I was a teenager. I guess I was trying to relive some of those youthful memories. I grew up too fast and enjoyed

CHAPTER 5

slowing down and just being with someone whose company I enjoyed. I didn't see an issue with the age difference because we were not having an intimated relationship. She was sweet. What made that summer even better was that I wasn't drinking or doing drugs; I was just working and playing softball, living a normal life.

Then, two younger guys, brothers my age, joined the scene. They also worked at the supermarket in the summer, and we quickly became good friends. They were Jewish too. We all enjoyed the same movies and music, and our quirky senses of humor made hanging out a blast. Honestly, when I wasn't with Beth, I was chilling with these guys. I spent a ton of time at their place, and their parents really liked me. Robert, the older brother, went to the University of Pennsylvania, where his dad taught at Wharton Business School. If you're not familiar, Wharton is a big deal. It's where Donald Trump went to business school. Anyway, Rob's dad really took a liking to me and saw potential in me. He even said, "Randy, I can help you get into this school." I was like, "But I've never taken the SATs." He reassured me, saying it was all good. I mentioned I didn't have any money, and he was like, "No worries, there are grants, and you can stay with us in Pennsylvania while going to school with Rob." But I ended up passing on that chance, and I've regretted it ever since. To be honest, I just didn't have any confidence back then. I didn't think I was smart or capable. Others saw potential in me that I couldn't see in myself, and I let that opportunity slip away.

When that summer ended and they went back to Pennsylvania and Beth had gone home as well. I went back to my drinking and sleeping around. I took a part time job as a relief manager at two local movie theaters that were own by a Jewish family that owned all the major movie houses in the area. I worked two nights a week to give the manager a night off. I met a teenage girl who worked there named Claudine. Her father was a dentist. She had a big home on the mainland, and I used to stay with her now and then. It seemed her father was never home. One night she was having a party with a bunch of high school kids there. I vividly remember the song "Subdivisions" by RUSH being played one night. Isn't it weird the things you remember? The thing is I remember driving from the mainland to Margate, but I didn't have a car. I must have been using hers. Some memories are faint. I have little memory of how my many relationships ended. It's like the relationships just dissolved. A lot of my life between 18 and 25 is a blur. There was not a lot of sobriety in my life back then. It was a very self-destructive path I was on. You see just like an illness will have physical symptoms, so to does a soul that is ill. We receive wounds when we are young and most of us never deal with them. We ignore them. We mask them. We medicate them. I carried around wounds I received as a child for decades. It was not until many years later that I finally dealt with them. That comes later in the book. Like so many people, sex became one of the things that I used to mask my pain.

In 1984 my mother came to visit me in Margate. She decided that we were going to Atlantic City to fake another robbery. We went to the police station and said we had been robbed by two Black guys with guns. This was another insurance scam. This is my mother. I have never had a great relationship with either my mother or my sister. My grandmother was the only woman in my life that was a healthy positive relationship. Maribess as well but we lost touch after she and my uncle divorced when I was 19.

CHAPTER 5

Well, I got bored with Casel's and returned to the Boardwalk the following summer. One day while at work Beth comes to the office on the Boardwalk looking for me. I was inside and someone told me that there was a young girl here to see me. It was Beth! I was surprised to say the least. What are you doing here? How did you know where to find me? After chatting for a bit, we decided to have dinner together that evening. We went to Duke Mack's. It was a year before I met my wife, Felicia. I should have taken her somewhere else. I was teased mercilessly by my buddies and coworkers because she was so young. "Who's that, your daughter?" Here I am 23 with my teenage girlfriend. Well, we really weren't boyfriend and girlfriend anymore. Just friends catching up. The previous summer was such a departure from the madness I had known for so many years. I didn't know how to be normal. My mind was as damaged as the rest of me. But for one summer I felt like a normal person. I had a mad crush on Beth.

One of the funniest memories from that time was when I was out drinking and gambling at the Claridge casino near the boardwalk. Frank Gorshin, the guy who played the Riddler on the old BATMAN TV show, was at my Blackjack table. For those who might not know, he was a big deal in the '60s and '70s, doing comedy and impressions. Anyway, it was past two in the morning, and we were all shit faced, including Frank. There was this drunk woman who kept calling him George, thinking he was George Gershwin. After she messed up his name a few times, Frank finally snapped and, sounding like Kirk Douglas, shouted, "MY NAME'S NOT GEORGE!" He was really annoyed. But she just kept at it, and by then, Frank was apoplectic. He grabbed his chips and stormed off. What a night that was.

So, there was this one time when I was working as an OPC

at a souvenir shop, and guess who walks in? Dom DeLuise! I had no idea he was such a big guy until I saw him in person. Anyway, I started chatting with him and asked what he was up to these days. He jokingly said, "I just wrapped up a porno film." Without missing a beat, I shot back, "Oh really? What's it called, Return of the Sperm Whale?" Believe me, he was a whale of a man. He cracked up and seemed really impressed with my quick comeback. I've always had a knack for humor, probably picked it up from Bill, who was super funny and had a sharp tongue. DeLuise told me, "I like that. I'm going to use that in my act." We talked a little longer, then he shook my hand and headed out.

I ran into an old buddy of mine on the boardwalk who I hadn't seen in a couple of years. We first met ages ago when he was the head of security for a wealthy family that owned all the souvenir shops, not just on the Atlantic City Boardwalk but also in Las Vegas. This family was super rich and Jewish, and my friend Brett was the one keeping an eye on all their stores. It's '84, and Brett's now a rookie cop in Atlantic City. We bump into each other on the boardwalk and start chatting. He mentions he's looking for a roommate, and I'm like, really? We talked it over, and since I didn't have much going on, I decided to move back to Atlantic City.

So, I moved in with Brett, who had a nice two-bedroom place. Brett loved to party, so we hit the bars and clubs every weekend. I remember one Saturday night we went out and didn't come back until Monday. It was one of those lost weekends, you know? But we had a blast. Now, we move to the summer of '85. After all the drinking, I ended up with a bleeding ulcer and had to be rushed to the hospital. I drank Absolute vodka on the rocks back then. I spent a week in the hospital, got out, and

CHAPTER 5

went right back to drinking. During that time in '85, I also fell back into doing coke, gambling, and chasing girls. It was a wild ride at 23 or 24, meeting new girls almost every week. It was just one big party until one night in '85 when I met Felicia. To say I was a "Player" is putting it lightly.

There was this bar and restaurant on the boardwalk at the corner of California Ave called Duke Mack's, I mentioned it earlier, and it was only about 30-40 yards from our office. At that time, I was working as an OPC in our timeshare sales office, but I had stopped handing out coupons. Instead, I was the one approaching couples on the boardwalk to invite them to our sales presentations. We eliminated the Runner position. During our breaks, we'd stroll down to Duke Mack's for drinks, and after work, it was our go-to spot for food and drinks. On Friday and Saturday nights, they even had a disco with a DJ, making it the perfect hangout.

One night in 1985, three stunning young Black women walked in: Felicia, her best friend and coworker Rhonda, and another friend, Jocelyn. The moment I saw Felicia, I was like whoa, who is that? She seemed just as intrigued by me. We ended up chatting at the bar, and from that night on, we were inseparable. I stopped dating other girls because I really liked Felicia. We often hung out at Duke Mack's, but there was also another bar just a short walk away called Scanuccio's. They had amazing food, like veal parm subs, and we loved going there for drinks and music. Before I met Felicia in '85, things were pretty wild for me. I was dating multiple girls, one from each of our three offices on the boardwalk, and they had no idea about each other. As a matter of fact, one of the girls tried to dissuade Felicia from dating me saying I had no interest in Black girls. In reality I had no real interest in that girl.

Before I met Felicia, things were out of control. It was not unusual for me to stay out all night long several times a week and then go home only to shower and then turn around and go back to work. I could be very vengeful back then. I used sex as a weapon to get back at people. If I felt that someone was looking at me like they were better than me because they had money, I would sleep with their girlfriend. So, there was this guy named Al, one of the bosses. A very unattractive man. I realized quickly that the only reason these unattractive men had good looking women was because they had money. Turns out, his girlfriend, Annette, had a thing for me, and we ended up dating. When Al found out, he didn't fire me, but I could tell it bothered him a bit that I was with her. That pleased me. She wasn't the most popular person, but I saw something in her—there was a sweetness and innocence to her. She even introduced me to her parents. We enjoyed going for walks and chatting, and even though we never discussed our past traumas, I think we both felt that connection. Unfortunately, that relationship didn't last long, and then I met someone else.

There was this guy, Sam Rubin, who was supposedly the owner of the company. I'm not sure if he was just a front for the mob or what, but he was definitely in charge. Sam was in his 40s and not exactly a looker—kind of reminded me of Steve Lawrence, an old singer from back in the day. Anyway, Sam had a young girlfriend who was my age, half Puerto Rican and half Italian, and she was absolutely gorgeous. Her name was Dolece. She happened to be the roommate of Annette. She had dark hair, dark eyes, and dark skin, plus an amazing figure. She saw me outside of our office, and came over to start chatting with me. She was definitely trying to make a move. She confessed later that my blue eyes caught her attention. I could

CHAPTER 5

always tell by the way a woman would look at me that she was interested. There is a certain eye contact they make. I used to call it the 'goo goo eyes'. I asked her out, suggesting we hit up a bar after work. She was totally down for it, and we ended up going together. All my coworkers were jealous that night. She came back to my place, and we dated for a few months. We had some fun adventures, but things got pretty intense. We were both a bit unpredictable and hot headed, which led to some wild arguments. I remember being at the office, yelling at her on the phone while my coworkers looked on, shocked that I'd risk losing such a good-looking girl. Honestly, I didn't care. Then, a couple of months in, she dropped the bomb that she was pregnant and wanted an abortion. I had no say in it, and that pretty much ended things between us. I was fine with the breakup though; I was living the life of an international playboy with a bunch of girlfriends.

There was this one girl, Ingrid from Sweden, who Felicia couldn't stand. One night, while Felicia and I were still figuring things out, I was in a booth at Duke Mack's with Ingrid, feeling buzzed, and I bragged to my friend Abdeen that I was International. Before there was Pitbull, I was Mr World Wide. I was such an asshole back then. My confidence at times became arrogance. I was very cocky back then, and some women are drawn to that. But thankfully, I was about to leave that phase behind. Felicia and I spent the summer of '85 in Cape Cod together while I worked for a timeshare group there, and we had a blast.

Before Felicia I was a lose cannon. If I wasn't entertaining a young lady, I was in the casino losing my money. I had a bad gambling problem. I would make $1000 for the week and lose it an hour after getting paid. I would have to barrow some money and eat ramen noodles the rest of the week. It was not unusual for me to spend twenty-four hours straight in a casino. Wherever I was found in those days I had a drink in my hand, coke up my nose and a girl on my arm. From 18 to 24 I was off the rails completely with only short periods of normalcy like in 1983, the summer of Beth and the Brodo's.

We took a break from Atlantic City, from gambling, and from all the chaos that came with it. Sure, we'd have a drink here and there, but it was nothing compared to what I was used to. During that time, we really connected and fell in love. I was crazy about Felicia.

When summer wrapped up, we headed back to Atlantic City and took an apartment at Lighthouse Plaza on Atlantic Ave. So, we settled into our new life together. We went into housekeeping. Felicia was working as a salesperson for a timeshare company, and I was the marketing guy. I'll never forget this one incident at the office. There was a Roy Rogers a few doors down—kind of like a Burger King, but they've been out of business since the early '90s. Anyway, there was this young black girl who had a crush on me and would flirt a bit, but I wasn't interested since I was with Felicia and happy. Then there was this white guy who was totally into her, and he got super jealous. One day, he stormed over to me while I was chatting with a coworker outside our office. He started yelling, spitting everywhere because he was so worked up and drunk. I still had my old temper, and when he spat at me, I couldn't help it—I threw a left hook that sent him flying. He hit the ground hard, and they had to help him up and carry him away.

We ended up losing a lot of friends through the years. A lot of them fell victim to overdoses and drugs from our timeshare days. I can think of at least ten people right off the bat. Some

CHAPTER 5

went to jail, and others either died in there or from drugs after getting out. Then there was the death of Betty O'Neil. She was a sweet older lady that was killed by a drunk driver. Kenny and I were the only ones from the company that attended her funeral.

There's this one moment that's stuck with me—this guy named Steve. He was a big shot on the sales team, and thought he was the best thing since sliced bread. One day, I was chilling on the boardwalk, leaning against the railing by the beach, when I saw Steve walk into a smoke shop just a couple of doors down from our office. Next thing I know, he comes out with handcuffs on, being escorted by two FBI agents. Turns out he was involved in the drug trade, and they finally caught him. Honestly, it wasn't that surprising; we'd seen plenty of people get arrested before. The drug scene in the timeshare business back in the '80s was wild. Cocaine was everywhere.

When I first moved to Atlantic City in '82 and started as a runner for this timeshare company called First American Travel, I met this older guy named Abdeen. He was about 15 years older than me, a sharp-looking Black man with a medium complexion, super articulate, and smart. Abdeen was well-read and had a good grasp of the world. He became a mentor to me, seeing me as this young, naive Jewish kid, which I totally was. I was decent with girls, but that was about it. Abdeen and I became close; he was like a big brother to me. I got to know his whole family—met his mother, his brothers, and his daughter. He took me into the parts of town where White folks usually didn't go.

We used to go and score some drugs. We'd do this and that. He always had my back, teaching me stuff and helping me be a bit more street-smart. Abdeen was a close buddy, but he passed away too, from drugs. He died in the late '90s. The drugs and the drinking just got to him. In '83, I met this guy named Kenny. He was Jewish, and we're still friends. Kenny was a great worker, made a ton of cash, but he had a serious gambling issue. Back then, he was into a lot of coke and crank. But man, he had an awesome sense of humor, just like me. We hit it off quickly, especially since there weren't many Jewish folks in our line of work. Thankfully Kenny eventually put his bad habits behind him and married his long time girlfriend. Later in the summer of 1985, I had just returned from Cape Cod with Felicia. I was doing well financially. Abdeen and I were working together, and then Kenny joined us, so the three of us teamed up. We started doing marketing for about three different timeshare companies around the Greater Atlantic City area.

So, we were raking in some serious cash back then. I was pocketing $2,200 a week, which was a hefty sum for a 25-year-old in 1986. Instead of saving, which I was never great at, I decided to live it up. My buddy Abdeen and I would hit up Trump Plaza for breakfast, enjoying steak and eggs. After work, we'd swing by the fish market to grab swordfish, shrimp, and lobster tails. The song "Big Shot" by Billy Joel appropriately describes our mentality at the time. We felt like we were on top of the world, thinking the good times would never stop. But, of course, they did. Still, we had a blast until it all came crashing down. The gravy train would not last forever.

Felicia and I decided to get married in Las Vegas and the day before our flight, I found myself in a bit of trouble—I was arrested on the boardwalk. Back then, you needed a license to solicit, and for some reason, I didn't have mine that day. I ended up in jail, and Kenny had to come to my rescue and bail me out, struggling to find change since he only had $100 bills. It was a comedy of errors. I had to get out because we were flying to Vegas the next day. Given the cultural differences—Felicia being Black and me being White and Jewish—we decided it was best to elope, just the two of us, with my Uncle Sandy and his second wife, Rose, meeting us.

We stayed at Caesar's Palace. Our wedding took place at The Little Church of the West, right next to the Hacienda, which is long gone now. The church got moved next to that pyramid-shaped hotel, Luxor. It's a well-known spot where Elvis and other celebs got married. So, on September 26, 1986, Felicia and I got married.

Just before the wedding

Just married 9/26/86

We had a reception at her mother's place in Newark, New Jersey two weeks after the wedding. My mother, sister, grandmother and friends like Joe, Kenny, and John all showed up for the celebration. It was a great day—no drama, just good times. My relationship with my mother wasn't super close at that time, but it was nothing compared to what it would become. Now, I'm happily married to my wife, Felicia, still working in the timeshare industry, and it's time to turn the page to the next chapter.

Kenny, John, Felicia, myself and Joe

Chapter 6

I Will Always Love You

The song "I Will Always Love You," famously performed by Whitney Houston, holds a special place in my heart. Felicia knew Whitney Houston during her high school days as she lived in the same neighborhood. For this reason we followed her career closely. Whitney was ubiquitously on the radio and jukeboxes when Felicia and I started going together. Felicia's best friend, Rhonda, would marry the musical director for Whitney Houston's tour years later. The song perfectly captures Felicia's unwavering love for me, which began in 1985 and has never wavered. She embodies loyalty, love, and commitment, making that song incredibly meaningful to me. In 1986, I took a significant step in my life by getting married. You may be asking what she saw in me? Good question. She saw something and maybe there was a touch of the fixing the 'bad boy' going on? You'll have to ask her. I can tell you Felicia was always an independent strong woman. Her mother raised her to be that way.

Marriage changed me and made me more responsible. I mentioned earlier that I had an occasional gambling problem.

CHAPTER 6

One time shortly after we were married I lost about a thousand dollars in the casino. Felicia threatened me saying, if I did that again she would leave me. She was not one to make idol threats so I stopped gambling. That summer, as I mentioned earlier, I was collaborating with Kenny and Abdeen, and we had established a successful partnership, marketing for three different companies in Atlantic City. At just 25 years old, I was bringing home around $2,200 a week, and honestly, I had no idea how to handle it, so I often squandered it like I did with everything else. If I knew then what I know now right? Hindsight is 20/20.

The year 1986, the year of our marriage, turned out to be quite enjoyable. I was thriving on the boardwalk, making money, and relishing my new life as a husband, filled with amusing moments along the way.

A film titled *Wise Guys* was currently being shot in Atlantic City, and I vividly recall a day when I was strolling through Resorts Casino. It was there that I bumped into Captain Lou Albano. Naturally, I was quite familiar with Captain Lou from his time as a manager in the WWF; he was a household name. You might know him from the Cindy Lauper "Girls just want to have fun" video. He played her father.

I knew he had a fantastic sense of humor and was quite sharp, so I approached him and asked, "Captain, did you really write The Beatles' White Album and Abbey Road?" Without missing a beat, he turned to me, clearly aware of my playful setup, and replied, "Of course! I wrote those, along with Yellow Submarine and Sgt. Pepper."We spent a few minutes exchanging jokes and reminiscing about my love for wrestling. It was a delightful encounter.

New Years Eve at Duke Mack's 86/87

Felicia's mother had remarried a wonderful man named John several years before our marriage. He was kind, generous, gentle, and highly educated—a truly successful individual. Tragically, John fell seriously ill with hepatitis and passed away that April of 1987. I will never forget the day Felicia received the heartbreaking news from her mother. I had never seen her so devastated; all I could do was hold her and let her grieve. A few days later, we attended the funeral in North Jersey, where a family friend, a passionate Baptist preacher, delivered the sermon. While the preaching didn't change me that day, something remarkable happened a day or two later. I experienced an extraordinary spiritual moment; unlike anything I had ever felt before. It was as if God had entered the room and touched me, and in that instant, I realized that God and Jesus were real. In Evangelical terms, I suppose you could say that was the moment I was "Born Again." I had always believed that God existed, but this was personal.

CHAPTER 6

I picked up the phone and called my wife, unsure of how to express what I was feeling. I told her that I felt profoundly different, as if a weight had been lifted and everything had been cleansed. It was as if I had been given a fresh start, a rebirth of sorts. It's important to note that I didn't come from an Evangelical Christian background, so this kind of language was completely foreign to me. I was genuinely transformed; my life had taken a dramatic turn, and my friends could see the significant change in me right away.

A few months later, we received the news that Sam Rubin, the owner of the company where I had worked from 1982 to 1985, had passed away. He was a Jewish man, older than me but relatively young. He wasn't even fifty. He would always bum cigarettes from me and his death shocked me. I mentioned him earlier. I had stolen his girlfriend Dolece.

Then came 1988, the year my son Andrew was born on October 8th. He arrived six weeks early, weighing just 4 pounds and 15 ounces. I vividly remember sitting in the neonatal unit, where all the premature babies were cared for, when the Beach Boys' song "Kokomo" played on the radio. That song always brings me back to those moments, holding my tiny son in my hands and marveling at the fact that he was mine. Andrew had to stay in the hospital for a week because his lungs weren't fully developed, and I can still recall the heart-wrenching day we had to leave without him. Felicia was utterly devastated, her heart breaking as she cried. I felt sad too, not just for myself but especially for Felicia. He was my son and I loved him but for a mother to have to leave her new born child behind must be incredibly painful. Fortunately, after a week, we were finally able to bring Andrew home, and our joy was immense. He quickly started to gain weight once we were home, thanks to Felicia breastfeeding him, which proved to be much more effective than the formula he had in the hospital.

Becoming a father had a profound impact on me. I became very responsible at this point in my life and had every intention of being the best parent I could be. Fatherhood acted as a restraint, holding me back from the actions that were second nature to me in my youth. Now I'm a father. I have responsibilities. I have people depending on me. I had to grow up and did.

Let's turn our attention to 1989, a year that was particularly difficult for me. My mother sought to borrow money from my grandmother, but this time, my grandmother firmly said no. In the past, she had already given my mother a staggering amount—around $40,000, if not more. After being turned down by my grandmother, my mother approached my uncle, who also refused to help. Then, she came to me, asking me to co-sign a loan that was supposedly for my sister and brother-in-law to buy a house. I had no doubt that my mother was involved in this scheme and would benefit from it. I flatly refused. Why? Because I had just gotten married and was starting my own household, and I knew my mother had never paid a bill in her life. For the sake of brevity, I left out the many times bill collectors would call the house or the Sheriff would come to the door to serve papers related to unpaid debts. In the past she never repaid my uncle whenever he loaned her money. I wasn't about to jeopardize my credit for her. This refusal led my mother to sever ties with me, as well as with her own mother and brother.

The only family I had left, aside from Felicia and my son, were my uncle and grandmother. That year was also tough because I sent my mother pictures of my son in a card, only for her to return them, refusing to acknowledge her grandson. To

CHAPTER 6

this day, she has never met my children, nor does she show any interest in them. When she sent those pictures back, I was devastated, crying in our kitchen and asking Felicia, *"why does my mother hate me?"* It felt like a fresh abandonment, just as painful as when I was twelve. I couldn't comprehend how someone could be so cruel, and I began to refer to her as El Diablo in my mind. My sister staying true to form joined her in cutting off communication with me, my uncle, and my grandmother—all over what? Money! The love of money is the root of all of evil. I had no contact with my mother or sister for twenty years.

Later that year, a new figure will step into my life: a man named Tom Joseph. Tom was an incredibly successful businessman from Pennsylvania, specifically the Pittston area. If you've seen the movie The Irishman, Pittston is where Russell Bufalino was from. The Joe Pesci character in the film. Tom told me that he knew Russell and was friends with him. Tom became my mentor, guiding me in both business and personal matters. I joined his team and took on the role of vice president at his newly established marketing firm in Atlantic City, called Tidewater Marketing. One invaluable lesson he imparted, which has stuck with me ever since, is the mantra: Assume Nothing. Never assume that someone is going to follow through on things. To be successful sometimes you need to do your job and the others guys job. While it's impossible to handle everything on your own without exhausting yourself, delegation is key. However, Tom taught me that when you delegate, you often compromise on quality, as others may not meet your standards. Learning to accept this is crucial; otherwise, you risk burning out trying to manage every detail. The principle of assuming nothing has woven itself into the very fabric of my life. I have learned to be proactive and anticipate what others will do or not do. I have very strong survival instincts. Tom was a dear friend and a kind and generous man. Sadly he passed away in 2021 due to complications of COVID.

In 1990, on March 12th, my daughter Randee is born. Coincidentally, this day also marks the birthday of my mother-in-law Laverne and my former business partner Kenny, all sharing the same special date. It was a memorable day for me. To celebrate Randee's arrival, I took my 17-month-old son Andrew to Tony's Baltimore Grill in Atlantic City for pizza, a tradition I had started.

A few months later, while standing on the boardwalk, my friend Kenny approached me with the news that Sam Rubin had passed away. I responded right away, AGAIN! It turns out that when he passed away in 1987, it was to escape IRS prosecution. This time, he truly was gone. We shared a hearty laugh about my quick reply, a joke that Felicia and I still chuckle about today. You see, I had been surrounded by individuals of questionable character—alcoholics, drug users and dealers, liars, cheats, thieves, and even murderers. Initially, I fit right in, but then I became a Christian, and my moral compass shifted dramatically.

Later in 1990, the same year Randee was born, we moved to Georgia for a year. We chose that area because Felicia's sister lived nearby. We settled in Chamblee, Georgia, part of the greater Atlanta region, which was a lovely place. We began attending First Baptist Church, where Charles Stanley, a well-known pastor in the Evangelical community who sadly passed away a few years ago, led the congregation. We enjoyed our time there, and I tried hard to blend in and be a typical churchgoer, but I always found it challenging. No matter the church or its

CHAPTER 6

denomination, I struggled to feel like a true member of the community. Being a racially mixed couple and with me being Jewish, we always were different. We just never really fit in where ever we went. While we made friends wherever we went—Felicia and I were never shy about socializing—we still felt out of place in the larger picture. Looking back, I realize that much of the responsibility for that disconnect likely lies with me and my own issues, rather than any shortcomings of the church itself. Less than a year later, we returned to Atlantic City. Over the years, we attended various churches, and I noticed a pattern: about every three years, we would switch to a different one. There was always something off, something lacking, but I could never quite identify what it was. I was on a quest for something elusive, and it felt like no one had the answer.

As the story unfolded, I eventually grasped the reasons behind it all. For now, let's just say we moved from one church to another. Over time, I've come to see that Protestantism is steeped in post-Enlightenment thought—heavy on reason and logic but lacking in mystery. They treated the Bible like a textbook, and I've realized how inadequate that perspective can be. There's a song by Tears for Fears that resonates deeply with me, titled "No Small Thing," from their 2022 album, "The Tipping Point." One line particularly struck me: *"Reason gonna bind you, cripple, and confine you."* Hearing that lyric struck me because I recognized that my years in Evangelicalism were dominated by reason and logic, relying heavily on my understanding. This approach didn't bring fulfillment for me, nor did it for Felicia. She never accepted Reformed theology. It took me thirty years to catch up to her. She had it right all along.

1992 was a challenging summer for me. I had met a coworker

named Carol, who was hired as my assistant. She was a few years younger, married, and had a daughter, just as I was married with two kids. Carol was stunning, with long brunette hair. Before long, we found ourselves emotionally drawn to each other. We began meeting for breakfast before work and drinks after hours. Thankfully, it never escalated to a physical relationship, but I still carry shame for the emotional bond we formed. One incident that is significant to the story is the time Carol had a fender bender. She called the house looking for me. I was surprised she didn't hang up when I didn't answer and Felicia did. She told Felicia that she had an accident. Felicia knew who she was and in spite of that she offered for Carol to come to our place while she waited for the tow truck. That is the woman Felicia is. She is a saint. After several months, I ended the relationship. It was a dark time for me in which I found it hard to sleep. My conscience bothered me terribly. At that time, I felt a growing distance from Felicia; she seemed unhappy, and I sensed we weren't connecting. Looking back, I understand now that her feelings stemmed from being alone in our second-floor apartment, with no air conditioning and two toddlers to care for, all while her family lived over two hours away. She felt utterly alone. I am truly sorry and filled with regret for the hurt I've caused this incredible woman. In my self centered understanding of things, I never considered how the circumstances were effecting Felicia. I admit that I lacked empathy in those days. Thankfully I have developed empathy as the result of the many challenges that are to unfold in a few years.

In 1993, we made the decision to leave our apartment in Brigantine and move in with my mother-in-law, Laverne, in East Orange, NJ. We needed a fresh start. It was about a two-hour drive from the Greater Atlantic City area where we had been living, so Felicia, the kids, and I settled in with Laverne. Our personalities often clashed; she is strong-willed and very opinionated. However, I don't want to cast her in a negative light because she is one of the most devoted Christians and generous individuals I have ever met. She has financially helped us, our children, her children and countless others. Reflecting on our relationship, I realize that the issues I had with her stemmed more from my own unresolved wounds than from her actions. I struggled with strong women because my past experiences, particularly with my mother, had taught me to associate their strength with hurtful behavior. I'll delve deeper into this later.

Felicia with the kids in '94

CHAPTER 6

That same year, I took a job at a hotel in Short Hills, NJ, an affluent area known for its expensive homes and wealthy residents. The Hilton at Short Hills was a prestigious 5-Diamond property, recognized by AAA for its exceptional standards. I truly enjoyed my time there; the camaraderie with my colleagues was fantastic and made the work enjoyable. I was hired as a supervisor, working the door, overseeing the valets and working as a bellman a few days a week. It was a refreshing change from my previous role as vice president for Tom Joseph, where the job never seemed to end. Tom would call me as soon as I got home, and I'd find myself on the phone with him for hours.

I met a lot of celebrities working there. Most notably Joe DiMaggio, Muhammad Ali, Walter Payton, Arnold Palmer, Jack Nicklaus, Martin Landau, Michael J Fox and Phil Jackson. I met Christopher Reeve before and after his accident. He was receiving rehabilitation treatment at a nearby facility. This was after his riding accident where he broke his neck. He was living at the hotel with his wife and children. Joe DiMaggio had an aura about him that is hard to describe. It was exciting to meet such notable people.

We had a lot of regulars and very wealthy guests. One gentleman in particular used to dine several times a week at our upscale dining room. As the doorman I would look after his Rolls Royce and we got to know each other quite well. He was Jewish as well and that contributed to our friendship. He was a distinguished looking older gentleman who had white hair and wore thick black eyeglasses. One evening while he is on his way to dinner I said to him, "You look like Cary Grant." He replied, "He's dead." "That's what I mean" I shot back. We got a good chuckle out of that. I really loved working there. There were plenty of long days and headaches, but once my shift ended, I headed straight home. There was nothing left to discuss or ponder. That was simply it, and I cherished that simplicity.

However, later that year, something truly terrible occurred. My grandmother lived alone in the home where she had raised my mother and uncle. One afternoon, my grandmother was brutally attacked and robbed in her driveway which was hidden from the street by large shrubs. It's important to note that she owned some stunning, valuable pieces of jewelry, including a very large diamond ring that was stolen. The robber told my grandmother that he would kill her if she saw his face. This is a frail woman in her eighties mind you. I cannot imagine the fear that gripped her that day and that she must have lived with afterward being all alone in that big house.

Now, here's where I need to be careful. We suspected that my mother might have been involved. Why? Because of her history with previous thefts, shady dealings and constant need for cash. We were aware of the unsavory characters she associated with. Unfortunately, we had no eyewitness accounts, so my uncle and I could only voice our suspicions to each other. I have my thoughts about who was tasked with this deed. But really, what kind of person would do such a thing? The thought that my mother could orchestrate her own mother's robbery is chilling. I buried that memory and forgot about it for over 25 years until my wife brought it back to my mind recently. It's just dreadful, isn't it? Some things are too painful to acknowledge so we suppress them. But the wound is still there. The trauma is buried below the surface, eating away at our soul.

About a year later, Laura was diagnosed with a brain tumor, which led to her moving into a nursing home just a couple of miles away from her house on the Boulevard. This was the same

CHAPTER 6

nursing home where my great-grandfather spent a brief time before passing away, and where my grandfather had also stayed before his death. While we were living in New Jersey, I made it a point to drive up every week, usually on Sunday nights, to stay at the house. It was a two hour drive from work to her home. The following day, I would visit her at the nursing home. I kept this routine for over a year. Occasionally, I would go on a Monday night instead, mainly because Ernie's, my favorite pizza place in New Haven, was closed on Mondays but I could go on Tuesday.

In 1996, my grandmother moved to California to reside in an assisted living facility close to my uncle, ensuring he could visit her regularly and keep an eye on her well-being. For several years, I made it a point to fly out there annually to see her. Although I didn't have the funds for those trips, my uncle generously covered the costs. He was incredibly kind and understood the special bond I shared with his mother, which I believe he truly valued. He knew I would drive from New Jersey to Connecticut to visit her weekly, and I think he appreciated my efforts on behalf of his mother.

One memorable trip to California, Sandy took me to the Dog show in the Sacramento area, where my aunt Maribess was showing her dogs. Maribess was a boxer breeder and often showcased her dogs in competitions. She lived a few hours away in Truckee, near Lake Tahoe. That particular year, she was participating in a dog show in Sacramento, so my uncle decided to take me along for a long-awaited reunion with my favorite aunt, whom I hadn't seen in nearly two decades. As I approached her, she had her back turned, but before I could say a word, she spun around and exclaimed, "Randy!" She recognized me immediately, saying, "I know those eyes anywhere." I had striking blue eyes back then.

Later that year, after I returned to New Jersey, my uncle made the difficult decision to sell the family home since my grandmother was now in California. This was the house where my uncle and mother had all grown up, and I had a deep emotional connection to it that words can hardly express. All the sleepovers and family dinners. All the holidays together. It had always meant everything to me. It represented family, love, warmth, and joy. As a result, I cherish nothing but fond memories of that home. I recall a weekend trip from New Jersey to Connecticut to visit my uncle. Before he arrived, I took it upon myself to remove all the carpets— not just the area rugs, but the wall-to-wall carpeting as well. Everything had to be tossed into the large dumpster outside. We needed to clean the entire place, scrub the floors, and prepare it for sale. I often dreamed of having the money to purchase that house for my own family.

In 1994 we moved to Metuchen, a charming spot in Central Jersey, not far from Rutgers or Perth Amboy. In fact, the street we lived on was called Amboy Ave. Metuchen had a quaint, Mayberry-like vibe, reminiscent of the Andy Griffith Show. It was a small town with a true neighborhood atmosphere, far removed from the hustle and bustle of city life. The pace was relaxed, and we absolutely loved it. We settled into a lovely garden apartment with friendly neighbors, and the management was a kind, family-oriented group.

Throughout the years, we had always kept dwarf rabbits as pets. Felicia and I had started this tradition the year we got married. Now, in 1994, our little dwarf bunny named Chuck had an unfortunate accident and broke his leg. He had jumped into the rocking chair in the living room, a piece of furniture we bought when the kids were young, as Felicia would often nurse them there. Unfortunately, Chuck got one of his legs stuck in the slats of the chair. We rushed him to the nearby vet, just a quarter mile from our home, named Thom Pahdi. Dr. Thom was an incredibly intelligent man from India, not only a veterinarian but also holding a PhD in philosophy. He and his family were Brahmin, which refers to the highest caste in the traditional Hindu caste system. We quickly became good friends.

Thom discovered that he genuinely enjoyed our conversations. Thom was a convert to Christianity as I was. He was the first person to make me realize that I was intelligent, articulate, and engaging, as he would describe me. Our connection blossomed to the point where we began having lunch together weekly, a tradition that lasted over a year. We shared some truly enriching discussions. I believe individuals like Thom, who appreciate stimulating and thought-provoking dialogue, often struggle to find others who share that same enthusiasm. Some people perceive such conversations as too intense or lofty, and I understand that perspective. Some enjoy discussing people rather than Ideas. I try to avoid that as much as possible. Nevertheless, Thom and I cherished our time together. We enjoyed discussing religion and philosophy.

He was an incredibly kind and generous person. I recall a time when my car broke down, leaving me in a bind since my job at the Hilton was about half an hour away. Without hesitation, Thom opened his checkbook and offered me a check to help me purchase a used car. I hesitated, mentioning that it might take me some time to repay him, but he insisted, saying, "No payback necessary. This is a gift." His generosity was truly remarkable, and his kindness has always stayed with me. Both our families became quite close but over the years we lost touch. Geographical distance does that sometimes. Maintaining relationships takes great effort. I do my best to keep up with my New Haven friends. I often miss living there and being close to them.

Another beautiful aspect of this story is how it connected me with Jacob, a Pakistani man I met at the gas station where I frequently stopped late at night for fuel. In New Jersey, attendants pump your gas, and Jacob was always there. Originally born a Muslim, he later converted to Christianity and changed his name to Jacob. We developed a strong friendship, discussing our faith and beliefs, as well as his experiences in Pakistan. One night, after work, I pulled into the gas station and remembered that Jacob didn't have a car, despite being a skilled mechanic. I decided to bless him as I had been blessed by Thom. I decided to give him my old car knowing he could repair it. So, I said Jacob, here are the keys to your car. It's in front of my apartment. You can come and get it and take it and it's yours. Jacob started crying. He was so touched. I've never forgotten about that, and I've never forgotten about him. He introduced me to his wife and his children, and they were a very beautiful family. I hope he's doing well and look forward to seeing him again someday.

Around 1996, and my son Andrew is enrolled in a local Christian school. We were hesitant to send our kids to public school due to our concerns about the education system's output. However, living in a lovely neighborhood in Metuchen, with the elementary school just a couple of blocks away, we thought we'd give it a shot and let Randee attend kindergarten there. There were financial considerations as well as Andrew was in a private school and the added expense of another child in that school was beyond our budget. The first day, she came home with a

CHAPTER 6

pamphlet that said, "My Two Daddies." I turned to Felicia and said, "That's it; she's not going back." You see, I believe that parents should determine when and how to introduce sensitive topics to their children, not anyone else. I didn't care what I had to do, both of my kids were going to private school. I took an extra job to make up for the financial shortfall. Felicia eventually went back to work during the day. I worked nights. She would come home from work and I would then leave for my job. We did this for years.

I share these stories and anecdotes to draw attention to the fact that each and every one of us is the product of our environment and upbringing. We come into the world a blank slate with no preconceived ideas or prejudices. No those things are taught. My views on homosexuality were shaped significantly by my upbringing. Born in 1961, my father served as a Marine, and during the '60s, being Gay was still largely hidden. Sure, there were Gay bars, but they were places where straight people generally kept their distance. It was a mutual understanding: you do your thing, and we'll do ours. My Evangelical background further intensified my feelings about homosexuality, as I was taught that it was not only socially unacceptable but also against God's will. Additionally, I have personal experiences that influenced my perspective; I was molested by an older male and faced propositions from older gay men between the ages of 14 and 17 on several occasions. So, it's understandable why I wasn't the most accepting person towards the LGBTQ community back then. However, over the years, my attitude has evolved. In the last decade, I've met many gay and lesbian individuals who have shown more kindness and generosity than many Christians I've known. My views have evolved over the years. Our experiences shape us; both the good ones and the bad. My views may have seemed bigoted in the past but a real bigot is one who refuses to change or be influenced by positive experience.

I know someone who has fully transitioned from male to female, and whenever I see her, I always give her a hug. She can live her life as she chooses, and that's perfectly fine with me. However, I do have some concerns. The idea that a child or 8 or 9 years old can make the decision to transition to another sex is very troubling. More about that later. It seems to me that the LGBTQ community is over represented in television and entertainment. If they make up only about 2 to 4% of the population—though I'm not sure of the exact figures—why do they dominate so much of the media? It feels like they're featured in 80% of shows, movies, and commercials. This creates an imbalance that I find unsettling. I want to clarify that I'm not anti-gay; I've moved past that. I simply want to be left alone, and I want kids to be left alone too.

I've made significant progress in my views towards various groups, including the LGBTQ community, women, and even those with face tattoos. I never understood the desire to mark up your face. What was Post Malone and Little Wayne thinking? I am quite confident that the majority of those who tattoo their faces will regret it in not too many years. The few people I know that have gotten them have confided in me that they do indeed regret getting them. But as a Libertarian I acknowledge their freedom to do it. While I may not share their choices, I respect their right to live their lives as they see fit. I recognize I still have some learning to do, and I hope for patience in return. We're all on our own journeys, aren't we? I'm not against anyone; I just don't feel the need to actively support or endorse every lifestyle. I believe in a live-and-let-live philosophy. I don't see

CHAPTER 6

many people advocating for my causes, so I don't think it's fair to expect me to support yours. Honestly, I just don't care that much. Why must you demand my approval? I have no need for anyone else to affirm me.

I share some of this with you to reveal how my attitudes were formed and the changes that came in time. I understand that my words might be misinterpreted, but that's a risk you take when you express your thoughts. Sometimes words become filled with vitriol and eventually turn to actions. Sadly, we are living at a time where the political rhetoric is white hot with hate for the opposition. Things have become too acrimonious. I can only hope we can return to the middle and once again work together seeking solutions that benefit us all. I am against violence in any form, especially when it comes to those who are minorities or different. I may not agree with someone but I'll be the first to come to your defense if someone is threatening you with bodily harm. There is no place for that. We need to return to the attitude that while I may not like your idea, I believe you are coming from a good place. Ideas have consequences and bad ideas have bad consequences. But we can't influence each other and learn from one another if we are convinced that those who hold to different views are inherently evil. We must restore our faith in each other or progress is impossible.

As I mentioned before, I firmly believe that it is the responsibility of parents to determine the appropriate time and manner to discuss topics related to homosexuality and transgender issues with their children. Personally, I prefer that kids remain unaware of any form of sexuality during their elementary school years. Shouldn't they be allowed to enjoy a carefree childhood? Why must they confront adult themes at such a young age? Maybe I am a strong advocate for childhood innocence because mine was stolen from me? Maybe I just have too much nostalgia for a simpler time when I was a child. You have a different perspective, that's your business. You can raise your children however you see fit, and I respect that. However, I also have the right to raise my children according to my beliefs.

Is it justifiable for a boy to change in my daughter's locker room simply because he identifies as a girl? Or to enter her bathroom and make her feel uneasy? Why are his feelings prioritized over those of my daughter or yours? Is it fair for a young woman who has dedicated her life to her sport to be outperformed by a male who claims to identify as female? Why do his feelings take precedence? Even when males identify as females, they often still exhibit patriarchal behaviors that dominate women. I cannot support that.

It seems that many people today have lost sight of the fact that children are not miniature adults. They think, reason, and act like children. It's absurd to believe that kids can make mature decisions about their sexuality at the age of eight. There's a reason why children can't obtain a driver's license until they turn 16; the part of their brain responsible for decision-making is still developing. You may disagree, and that's your choice, but despite the current climate we find ourselves in, the science supports my position.

I always found it frustrating to be told how to act in specific settings, whether in school or at work. I've always considered myself a free thinker with a bit of a rebellious streak. I am not the type to jump on the band wagon. More often than not, whatever trend is being shoved down our throats today will be thrown out the window in a short period of time.

Sometime in 1995 I stumbled upon Calvary Chapel. This non-denominational church movement, which has a presence across the country, can be likened to a charismatic version of Baptists who embrace Dispensational eschatology. I won't delve into the details of that, as it's not essential. What truly mattered to me at Calvary Chapel was the opportunity to teach Bible studies. I initiated a Monday night class focused on apologetics, where I explored topics like evolution, creation, and various religions. It was during this time that I realized I had a gift for public speaking. Not only was I able to run my class as I saw fit, but I was also invited to address a few Sunday evening services. I was developing a small following and my opinion was being sought out by those who attended my classes.

Calvary Chapel was a sizable congregation, drawing around 1,000 attendees for Sunday services and about 300 for the Sunday evening ones. Speaking to such large crowds never intimidated me; in fact, I relished the experience. During this period, I developed a keen interest in the young earth movement, which posits that the earth is only 6,000 to 10,000 years old. To be honest, I'm not certain about the earth's age—whether it's thousands, millions, or billions of years old—and I've come to realize that it doesn't really matter. The core message of the Bible emphasizes not how or when creation happened, but who created it: God Almighty.

I became deeply involved in the young Earth movement and developed relationships with individuals at a ministry focused on young Earth creationism located in Kentucky. They were quite impressed with my work after I sent them recordings of my classes and Sunday evening talks. This led to an invitation to visit their headquarters in Kentucky, where I spent an entire day getting to know them and engaging in discussions with several high-ranking officials at the ministry. After about four hours of conversation, they offered me a position. They wanted me to relocate to Kentucky with my family to work as one of the top speakers' assistant, managing his schedule and speaking at local schools and small events to see how things would unfold. My wife, however, had some reservations about moving to Kentucky due to the prevalent racism in the area. While Kentucky is a beautiful state, we had encountered our share of racial issues, both outside and within the ministry. I vividly remember finding a book left on my desk that argued against interracial relationships, claiming they were sinful and contrary to God's will. Additionally, a young woman approached me for a conversation, expressing her confusion about the mixed messages she received from her pastor and parents regarding biracial individuals and relationships.

She shared that her pastor and parents have been sharing their thoughts about mixed-race individuals and biracial children, going on and on about it. However, I find you all to be genuinely kind, which leaves me feeling a bit perplexed. All I could do was be a friend to her and show her what normalcy looked like—what else was there to do? Our church was located across the Ohio River in Cincinnati, and it's important to note that during the era of slavery, crossing into Ohio meant freedom. The contrast in how we were treated in Cincinnati compared to Northern Kentucky was striking. In Ohio, we faced far less racism than we did in Kentucky. After about nine or ten months in Kentucky, we decided it was time to move on. My wife was unhappy, and our kids struggled to make friends. It just felt like the right moment to leave.

As I've matured I have left behind interest in partisan issues. Things that cause needless division. There is too much arguing over small details that are inconsequential. For people who believe that God created everything to divide over when he did it seems foolish and juvenile to me now. But those are fighting words to many people. There is an old adage that says, In essentials unity, in non essentials liberty, and in all things charity. I try to live by that now.

So, in 1998, we packed up and headed to Florida. The reason for choosing Florida was that my wife's mother lived there, and her brother also. So, our family, along with Felicia's mother and brother, all ended up in the same community in South St. Pete. We arrived in Florida, and my first job was at a call center for the cellular division of Capital One, which was then called America One before it went out of business. I spent a couple of years there, starting in inbound sales and eventually moving up to the retention department, which was initially based in Virginia but was newly established in the Tampa Bay area. They built it up from the ground.

They constructed an expansive campus featuring three buildings, a basketball court, a gym, and a cafeteria that was truly exceptional. It was impressively designed. I began my journey in the retention department at America One, all while grappling with personal challenges. This year, I lost my grandmother, who was 88, and it hit me hard. I cherished her deeply, and it made me reflect on my situation. I was beginning to face some health issues as well. I confided in my supervisor, expressing my doubts about continuing in my role. I explained that while I understood that the calls I received were from a small fraction of dissatisfied customers—around 3-5% of our total base—they represented 100% of my interactions. My job was to address their grievances, but I felt overwhelmed with my own issues. The burden felt immense.

After my grandmother's passing, we drove to Connecticut for her funeral. We couldn't afford flights, so I packed Felicia,

Randee, and Andrew into our compact Escort for the trip. My uncle kindly covered our hotel expenses, and it was heartwarming to stay together. He and his wife occupied one room, while the rest of us shared a spacious suite with several bedrooms. We gathered in the large living area, playing games, chatting, and laughing, creating cherished memories during that difficult time. It was nice to see my cousins again. My mother did not attend Laura's funeral.

Now it's 1999, and I'm still with America One. Over the years I would work for Capital One, Chase and Verizon Wireless in their call centers. My daughter's best friend lives in New Jersey, and they've maintained their friendship. She expressed a desire to visit her friend, and I agreed. My daughter has always had a flair for the arts—music, dance, theater, and film are her passions. I, on the other hand, have never been particularly artistic.

I've never really considered myself an artsy person; my strengths have always leaned more towards the intellectual side. However, I've managed to blend my emotions with my thoughts over time, creating a better balance. One particularly memorable experience I crafted for my daughter, Randee, stands out. We traveled from Florida to New Jersey so she could visit her friend, and one afternoon, I suggested that Randee and I head into the city. She had no idea what I had planned, and as we drove to New York City, excitement filled the air. We strolled around Broadway, taking in the iconic theaters she had only seen in magazines. We stopped for a bite at a deli right across from the Majestic Theater, where "Phantom of the Opera" was playing—her absolute favorite show at the time. I turned to her and said, "Let's see if we can take some pictures inside." She skeptically replied, "Dad, they won't let us in." Then, I revealed two tickets for "*Phantom of the Opera*"

CHAPTER 6

from my coat pocket and handed them to her, saying, "Maybe these will change their mind." Her joy was overwhelming, and tears of happiness filled her eyes. We entered the theater and experienced an unforgettable performance of the show. That day became a cherished memory for both of us. I may not have been the perfect father, but I always aimed to create special moments for my kids. I remembered how significant family trips to Disneyland were for me as a child, and I made it a point to share similar experiences with my own children.

I took them to Orlando for WrestleMania 24, knowing how much they loved wrestling, a passion I had introduced them to when they were around 11 or 12. They quickly became fans, and it created a strong bond between us that I cherish deeply. We even flew to Houston for WrestleMania 25, where The Undertaker faced Shawn Michaels in what many consider the greatest WrestleMania match ever. Being there for that instant classic was truly special. My lifelong love for wrestling started in 1973 when I was about 12, with the Worldwide Wrestling Federation, which later became the World Wrestling Federation, and eventually evolved into World Wrestling Entertainment.

At WrestleMania 24 Ric Flair retired. My training partner at the time was Jerry Sags, a retired professional wrestler. Jerry gave me a pair of front row tickets to RAW the night after WrestleMania 24. Jerry was part of the tag team known as The Nasty Boys with Brian Knobs. They were tag team champions in both WCW and WWF. Jerry was a great guy. He and his son would come over to our house to watch wrestling with us. It was a special experience to have a professional wrestler, who was a champion, hanging out at our place.

Randy Orton, one of our favorite wrestlers, used to do his signature pose where he stood on the ring post and raised both arms above his head. During the show, my son was seated a little higher up, and while Randy Orton was doing his pose, I decided to do it too. Randy Orton saw me in the front row and broke character to smile at me. My son reminded me of that moment recently, and it's a memory I still treasure. At that RAW, Ric Flair had a retirement ceremony. When RAW went off the air, The Undertaker, my favorite wrestler, came out to pay tribute to Ric Flair. We all went crazy.

We used to go to wrestling every week when FCW was in Tampa. That stood for Florida Championship Wrestling. It eventually became NXT which is on TV every week from Orlando. Back then in 2009 I weighed 237 and everyone at the arena assumed I was a wrestler. I was huge back then, with 18 inch arms and wore a size 46 suit.

These moments, from wrestling excitement to personal milestones and time with family and friends, have deeply shaped my life. Each memory brings a sense of joy and gratitude for the people and experiences that have been part of my journey. Our kids don't live with us anymore, but they come over and watch all the WWE PPV's with me.

CHAPTER 6

Myself with Hulk Hogan

Chapter 7

Losing my Health and More

Moving on to the year 2000, and I found myself working for a new company called Open Network. This tech firm specialized in software development, particularly considering the emerging HIPAA regulations that were becoming crucial for businesses that were healthcare related. Companies needed specific software to ensure their websites complied with these regulations, and that's where we came in. My role involved reaching out to businesses nationwide to gauge their interest in a product demonstration, which I would conduct online. If they were intrigued, a field salesperson would follow up with an in-person demo to seal the deal. These were significant contracts, often worth tens of thousands or even hundreds of thousands of dollars, focusing on enterprise solutions. Eventually I would be laid off as the company would downsize after September 11th, 2001.

However, while I was working there in 2000, I began experiencing unusual symptoms. My legs felt incredibly heavy, making it increasingly difficult to walk. I started to feel sudden electric shocks in my shins, which left me bewildered. To make

CHAPTER 7

matters worse, my face would occasionally go numb. I consulted several neurologists, but none could provide a diagnosis. The first one dismissed my concerns, suggesting it was all in my head, reminiscent of a faith healer who blames the patient for their own inability to heal. Because he couldn't find a cause, he simply attributed it to my imagination. Frustrated, I sought a second opinion from another neurologist who acknowledged that something was indeed wrong but couldn't pinpoint what it was. She referred me to Shands Hospital in Gainesville, FL, a reputable facility akin to the Mayo Clinic. After spending hours undergoing various tests and examinations, the neurologist returned with a diagnosis: I had some form of radiculopathy and atrophy in my right calf. While he recognized my issues, his advice was to simply learn to cope with it, and if I struggled, I should seek psychiatric help. This was the conclusion I received after 18 months of enduring this ordeal. This was unacceptable considering I had demonstrable neurological deficits accompanied by abnormal blood work.

A month later, my condition worsened to the point where I could barely walk, prompting a visit to the emergency room. Unfortunately, the nurse treated me poorly, questioning my presence and implying I was exaggerating my symptoms. It was disheartening to think that my unique illness was overlooked. Ultimately, I left the emergency room with no resolution, but they did manage to schedule me with one of the leading neurologists in Saint Petersburg within a week. In 2002, I met with Dr. Vasquez, nearly two years into my struggle with undiagnosed symptoms. Dr. Vasquez and I formed a bond as he would be my neurologist for over twenty years. He conducted nerve conduction studies, blood tests, and reviewed the results of a previous lumbar puncture. That same afternoon,

Dr. Vasquez delivered the news: I was dealing with two distinct diseases.

One of my conditions is Myasthenia Gravis, a neuromuscular disorder that targets the neuromuscular junction, the critical point where nerves communicate with muscles. This communication is essential for muscle contraction; without it, the muscles weaken significantly. Additionally, I was diagnosed with chronic inflammatory demyelinating polyneuropathy (CIDP), which is somewhat akin to multiple sclerosis as it damages the myelin sheath of the peripheral nervous system. I was informed that there was some central nervous system involvement as well. To visualize the myelin sheath, think of it as the rubber insulation on an electrical cord, protecting the wire inside, which represents the nerve. When this protective layer is compromised, it disrupts nerve signals, leading to sensations of shock. Over time, the nerves can be severely damaged, resulting in a complete loss of feeling and function in various parts of the body. This has been my experience. Myasthenia gravis has remained relatively stable over the years, but CIDP has progressed, causing me to lose more sensation in my hands, arms, feet, and legs over the past two decades. Currently, I estimate that I have only about 25% of the feeling left in my hands, which has severely impacted my dexterity. I have lost a lot of feeling in my feet as well which has effected my balance. Writing has become a challenge, and my handwriting is quite messy due to this condition. In 2007, I was also diagnosed with psoriatic arthritis, adding to my existing osteoarthritis that affects my neck, back, knees, and shoulders. This new diagnosis has been particularly damaging to my fingers, hands, and elbows. I have tried several biologic treatments such as Enbrel and Remicade without success, leaving me to cope with

CHAPTER 7

the persistent pain. Due to another health issue, I will discuss shortly, I am unable to take anti-inflammatory drugs like Motrin or ibuprofen, as they can lead to bleeding.

I'll share more details shortly, but first, let me take you back to 2003, the year I transitioned to full disability. Prior to that, I had been on short-term disability for several months and had attempted to return to work part-time at Verizon Wireless. However, after a few months, I realized I simply couldn't keep it up. Autoimmune diseases can be incredibly debilitating, leading to a level of fatigue that is truly overwhelming. It's not something you can just shake off with a cup of coffee; there's a real biological struggle happening within your body. So, I found myself on full disability. In the near future I would also be diagnosed with Hashimoto's disease, which is a thyroid disease. The symptoms of four autoimmune diseases can be confusing because they can overlap making diagnosis difficult at times. Having had to deal with them for so long now I can discern which disease is causing a particular symptom.

In 2004 we began attending a new church called Grace Christian Fellowship. This was a Presbyterian Church, steeped in reformed theology. What does that mean? Essentially, it's the belief in God's absolute sovereignty, suggesting that every event in life, from graduating college to the tragic loss of a child, is part of God's will. Moreover, it posits that God chooses certain individuals for salvation while others are left to face eternal damnation. This was a perspective I had accepted in the '90s, but I now see it as a profound misunderstanding of God's true nature. At that church, I met a young man named Arin Hatfield, who has been a cherished friend for the past 20 years. Despite the distance that grew between us when he moved to Denver, we've maintained our friendship. I hold him dear, and he has a wonderful family.

The following year, in 2005, marked my first major surgery, known as a thymectomy. The aim of a thymectomy is to excise the thymus gland, with the hope that this procedure will impede the progression of Myasthenia Gravis and prevent me from becoming severely incapacitated by the condition. Now, nearly two decades later, I can confidently say that the surgery was effective, as my Myasthenia has remained relatively stable and in remission for the most part. However, this was no minor operation; they opened me up as if I were undergoing open-heart surgery, completely transsternal, to extract the thymus from behind my breastbone. I was initially expected to stay in the hospital for 2-3 days, but due to complications, I found myself in the ICU for a week. It seems that every time I undergo a surgery or procedure, complications arise. I often find myself in that unfortunate 1% statistic—where they say, "Only 1% of people experience this," while everyone else is fine. Memories are faint but I do remember screaming in agony after the surgery.

So, moving forward, I recovered, and by 2007, I began to struggle with the theology of my church. We eventually transitioned to another Presbyterian Church that upheld Reformed teachings but they were more extreme. Then, a significant event occurred: the devastating tsunami that hit Indonesia in 2004. Over 200,000 human beings perished as a result of its devastation. During our men's Bible study, some men expressed the belief that those affected didn't matter to God or anyone else because they were not part of the elect and were predominantly Muslims. I went home that day, deeply troubled, thinking, "This can't be right." It struck me that the notion of God disregarding the lives and suffering of those deemed non-elect was fundamentally flawed. I have since learned that we become like what we worship. If your "god" is unfeeling and loveless, you will be the same.

This realization led me to leave Protestantism and return to Catholicism, where I found the belief that God loves everyone. Although their view of "Original Sin" would become a problem for me in the future. That is the belief first espoused by St. Augustine that each person is born into the world a sinner as guilty as Adam. The idea that an individual could be guilty of the sin of another is flawed. This was not taught until the fourth century but has become the default position of all Western Christianity, be it Protestant or Catholic, with a minority of dissenters. It is contrary to Judaism and *not* taught in the Tanach (Old Testament). What *is* taught in the Tanach is *"The one who sins is the one who will die. The child will not share the guilt of the parent"* Ezekiel 18:20. The early church, following the Jews which came before, believed that all are born innocent. Being human we are born with a propensity towards sin influenced by the world around us. The Orthodox call this "Ancestral Sin." Remember the lyrics from That's the Way of the World? *"Child is born with a heart of gold. Way of the World makes his heart so cold."*

Around this period, as I stepped away from Protestantism, Arin followed suit. He chose to embrace Eastern Orthodoxy and shared his thoughts with me, but I ultimately decided to return to the Roman Catholic Church. Since I had already been baptized, it felt like the simplest option. All I needed to do was walk through the door, and they would welcome me back. Later that year Felicia and I had a second wedding ceremony in the Roman Catholic Church, marking wedding #2.

At this time, both of our children were enrolled in a dual

program. This meant that while they were completing their studies, which included a mix of Christian schooling and home-schooling, they were also on track to earn associate degrees from the nearby St. Pete College. By the time they graduated high school, they would hold both a high school diploma and an Associates degree. However, an incident occurred at the college, which was conveniently within walking distance of our new home in Seminole, just about half a mile away. One day, my daughter faced a troubling situation at school when an older Black student began to harass her. She came home and confided in me, prompting me to accompany her to school the next day. When we arrived in her classroom, she identified the student. My heart sank as I took in his imposing figure—around 6' 2" and 230 pounds of muscle. I was no lightweight myself, standing at 5' 11" and weighing 220, but I knew he was younger and likely quicker. Nevertheless, I felt it was my duty as a father to confront him. I approached the young man and said, "Listen, my daughter has told me you're bothering her. We both find that unacceptable. Don't make me have to come back here again." He replied, "Yes, Sir, I understand." My daughter later assured me that he would never trouble her again.

    A few years down the line, at USF, a professor began to harass her, but my wife chose not to inform me, knowing how I would react. I would have taken drastic measures against that guy, but she didn't want her husband and the father of her kids behind bars. It wouldn't have been just a simple confrontation in the parking lot after class. No, I would have tracked him to his home multiple times, observing his surroundings. He would have been completely blindsided. My family means everything to me, and I always defend those who are vulnerable or mistreated. People who have been abused either become

CHAPTER 7

abusers themselves or protectors. I became a protector.

Chapter 8

House of the Rising Sun

2010 was a year that turned out to be quite challenging. I have titled this chapter *"House of the Rising Sun"* after the song by that title. It tells the tale of a man who followed a woman to his own ruin and loss. The lyrics are, *"There is a house in New Orleans, they call the Rising Sun. It's been the ruin of many a man. And God, I know, I'm one."* That year, I connected with a girl on Facebook. She was very attractive and twenty years younger than myself. Out of respect for my wife, I won't disclose her name; I'll simply refer to this woman as "her." She was from North East India where the people are very Asian in appearance. She was living in Israel working as a caretaker. Our initial interaction took place on a Catholic page where we discussed our faith. After a few weeks, she asked if she could call me, and I thought it was a harmless request. I had no idea what was about to unfold. When she called, we chatted, and her gentle, kind demeanor drew me in. She spoke very softly.

Felicia and I were experiencing some tension in our relationship. During this period, Felicia was a little harsh. Before I knew it, I was speaking with her on the phone nearly every day.

CHAPTER 8

I started drinking heavily and taking pills. On a few occasions I took pills and went out drinking and one night Felicia and my son went out looking for me. I was staggering home, drunk with no shirt on and bleeding from the knees from falling down. They stuffed me into the car and brought me home. I'm fortunate that I didn't get hit by a car crossing the very busy street the bars were on. I was a fucking mess. Not just that night but constantly. It was a very dark period for me. I had totally lost my way and was falling into a deep dark hole that would take years to emerge from.

She would reach out to me, even in the dead of night on her end, living in Israel. We would talk on the cellphone and over Skype, sharing our thoughts whenever the house was quiet— when the kids were at school, Felicia was at work, or was busy at school to become an X-ray technician. But then several months later, Felicia discovered something troubling. She had been secretly monitoring my activities, installing software on our computer to track my keystrokes. This was Felicia's moment of deepest betrayal. She caught me sending heartfelt messages to another woman, professing my love and desire to marry her. I can still recall Felicia's reaction, confronting me with, "What do you mean you want to marry her? You're married to me!"

The fact that Felicia was attending school to become and X-ray technician while all this is going on is not to be overlooked. It speaks to her strength as a woman. She managed to finish school, graduate and secure a position in her chosen field.

I had broken my vows, betrayed my family, and the weight of it all plunged me into emotional turmoil, prompting me to seek help from a psychiatrist. I was a mess. He conducted various tests, including IQ assessments, and discovered that my mind operated at a very fast speed, which often left me frustrated with others who took longer to express themselves. I often have the answer while the question is still being asked. I realized I needed to cultivate more patience, a skill I'm still working on. He informed me that my IQ was above normal as well, and may have been higher had I not been under such duress. The psychiatrist also noted my significant emotional distress, pointing out that my survey responses indicated I was desperately seeking help.

Although I hadn't mentioned it before, I did battle severe depression and thoughts of suicide over the years. There were many low points where I felt like giving up. I battled thoughts of being unworthy of life itself. My self image was poor. I saw myself as a worthless piece of shit. At times I thought, my wife and children would be better off without me. I thank God that I never carried through with those dark thoughts. But they were there. Feeling hopeless is an awful thing. The bible says that weeping may endure for the evening, but joy comes in the morning. Sometimes the night seems so very long, but the sun will rise again. Light will dispel the darkness. You just have to hang on to hope.

In 2011, after 25 years I was ending my marriage. As I mentioned we met on Facebook and soon began talking on the phone. Between the time I met her online and the time I went to Israel was about nine months. We spoke almost every day on the phone for two to three hours. By the time I got to Israel, we really knew each other well. Just as I had done in 1992 with Carole, I had formed another emotional relationship. From my point of view, I had my reasons and feelings of being neglected by my wife, but this was still wrong. I should have agreed to go to counseling to mend and resolve whatever issues we were having, whether real or imagined by me. Instead, I went to

CHAPTER 8

Israel to be with my new girlfriend.

The memory of Felicia's tears and the pain etched on her face when I left is something I will never forget. Strangely enough, as I prepared to leave for the airport, bound for New York and eventually Israel, a deep ache gripped my own heart, as if a dagger had pierced it. The pain was overwhelming, and I found myself questioning why I didn't just turn back, plead for forgiveness, and stop this madness. I was lost in my thoughts, unsure of my next move. So I made the leap to Israel, keeping in touch with Felicia sporadically during my time there. My mind was a mess. Emotionally I was in turmoil. All I thought about was myself, my happiness. My conscience was overwhelmed with guilt.

My first home was in Netanya, a stunning area right by the Mediterranean. I lived in a high-rise that was part hotel, part condo, and the view from my window was breathtaking. Initially I only saw her one night a week, from Saturday afternoon to Sunday evening, which was when we would go out for drinks or dinner. That was her only time off besides a few hours of free time daily. Yet, she sensed the temporary nature of our situation. She remarked that it felt like I was on vacation. While I had feelings for her, deep down, I still loved my wife. I cherished my time in Israel, but I couldn't bring myself to permanently leave my family behind. Eventually, I moved to Haifa, a place I grew to really love. I moved there because her job had moved her from Netanya to Haifa.

My view in Netanya

I spent over a year living in Haifa, an area also known as Mount Carmel. It's a place steeped in biblical history, particularly with the story of the prophet Elijah in First Kings. During my time there, I visited a church called Stella Maris, believed to be the site of The Cave of Elijah, and attended mass several times. Back then, I enjoyed drinking Guinness and Jack Daniels, which was quite pricey at around 300 shekels a bottle—more than double what it costs in the U.S. Occasionally to save money I would drink Israeli vodka because it was cheaper.

My favorite hangout was a lively spot called the Irish House, which was surprisingly popular in Israel. They often hosted bands from Ireland, and the atmosphere was electric. One of my fondest memories from the Irish House was college night on Mondays, where students enjoyed significant discounts. The place would be packed with students from the Technion,

CHAPTER 8

Israel's equivalent of MIT. I remember one night vividly when girls danced on the bar while we belted out Linkin Park songs together. That was not the usual atmosphere and it all happened very organically. Another place I frequented was Charlie's, just down the street. It had a modern vibe, filled with young people and rock 'n' roll music, but I always felt a bit anxious navigating the narrow staircase upstairs to the bathrooms, especially since it lacked a railing.

I emailed Felicia late in 2011 from Israel to tell her I thought I had a drinking problem. Looking back over the years Alcohol was a bigger problem for me than I had previously realized. I was lonely and filled with regret. I was not quite ready to end my relationship with "her", but I knew it was a matter of time. We were star crossed lovers from the start. From what I've read most middle-aged me have fantasies about running away with a younger woman, but most aren't foolish enough to actually do it. I can't say this was a mid-life crisis as my age didn't bother me. I had my hair. I was going to the gym and was in better shape than most that were thirty. I can remember sitting at the bar at The Irish House for my 50th birthday thinking to myself, I don't want to be a lonely drunk sitting at a bar with no family at 60 years old. I had known too many drunks during my life. I did not want to be one myself. Old, sad and lonely. In my heart I wanted my wife and family back. I knew I fucked up but had to believe this could be reversed somehow and made right. I had to hold onto hope.

Even after all these years, I've kept in touch with several friends from the Irish House through Facebook, watching them get married and start families. It's heartwarming to see how everyone is doing, especially since I returned home in 2012. Now, years later, I still cherish those beautiful, peace-loving people and miss both them and Israel dearly. They appreciate my support for Israel and my defense of her during times of unrest.

When I left Israel in March 2012, I knew in my heart that I would never see her again. After 14 months in Israel, I was ending the relationship that began in June 2010. The way I left it with her was I'll call you when I get settled. We continued to speak for a few months occasionally, but we both knew it was over. She knew it. I knew it. I was relieved to be honest. It was a relationship born in adultery and I knew it was wrong. I learned long ago that those who will lie *for* you will lie *to* you. How could I trust her? How could she trust me? I was lying to everyone in the beginning. Lying is too much work. It's hard to keep your stories straight.

I had a little narcissistic personality disorder going on during this period. If my wife had done to me what I had done to her, I would have gone crazy. I would have exploded in rage. But because I was the one doing it, it was OK. That's twisted. That is narcissistic. Thankfully my personality has recovered, and I have more empathy and am less selfish. The deceit and darkness of the human heart to be guarded against with most vigilance. The Proverbs in the Bible warn about the adulterous woman. She will lead you on the path to total loss and brokenness. I failed to heed those warnings.

She was a home wrecker, and I've decided to leave her behind in my past. I realize I could have said no; she chased after me, and I should have just blocked her on Facebook to end it. I can't place all the blame on myself though. My wife pointed out that once she knew I was married, she should have respected that boundary. That's a valid point. It was a failure on multiple levels, and it stands as perhaps the greatest moral failing of my

CHAPTER 8

life. It was a truly low moment where I betrayed and hurt those I care about the most.

Reflecting on my time in Israel, I find it difficult to delve into those experiences as they are filled with shame and regret. When I think of Israel now, my thoughts are more about the friendships I formed rather than the past with "her". One significant experience was my visit to Yad Vashem, the Holocaust Museum in Jerusalem. It was an incredibly impactful place, with well-curated exhibits that, surprisingly, left me feeling uplifted rather than despondent. However, there was a poignant moment when I entered my family surname, Pitkin, into the hall of records and discovered many entries of victims, all tracing back to Russia, the homeland of my ancestors. That was very sobering.

Some refer to it as the Shoah, a term synonymous with the Holocaust. The museum's logo, resembling a piece of barbed wire with a new leaf sprouting from it, symbolizes the emergence of new life from such a dark history. The Insignia truly showcases the spirit of the Jewish people—ever hopeful. Jews are a resilient and optimistic people, having faced persecution for millennia. I have my own thoughts on why this persecution and resilience exists, but perhaps I'll save that for my next book.

I was raised with strong Zionist values, heavily influenced by my grandfather, a staunch supporter of Israel. My grandparents lived through the Holocaust years during World War II, which instilled in them the importance of having a safe haven for the Jewish people. My own family has roots in Russia, where we faced persecution and pogroms, leading us to seek refuge elsewhere. Having a secure place for our people has always been crucial. As I've mentioned before, every Jew doesn't live in Israel but Israel lives in every Jew. I've always felt a deep connection to the Holy Land. The moment I stepped off the plane in Tel Aviv, it felt like home. While I was there I became an Israeli citizen. Even though I am not living in Israel anymore, I established a close bond with the land and the people. Although my Hebrew was limited at first, I learned enough to get by. I loved being there, even if I was drawn there for all the wrong reasons.

Another remarkable place I visited was the Western Wall in Jerusalem, the remnants of what was once the Temple Mount, home to the Second Jewish Temple. It stands as the holiest site for Jews worldwide. I also explored the Church of the Holy Sepulcher, revered as the holiest site for Christians, believed to be the location of Jesus's crucifixion and burial. I'll never forget the day I wandered through this sacred space. As I strolled around, I stumbled upon a grand structure that I didn't recognize. A tall, dignified man was nearby, and I approached him to ask, "Sir, what is that?" With a voice as deep as James Earl Jones, he replied, "That is the tomb of Jesus." I was utterly amazed. These experiences remain some of my most cherished memories from my time in Israel.

Chapter 9

Break the Man

The song "*Break the Man*" by Tears for Fears, from their 2022 album "The Tipping Point," addresses significant challenges I've faced emotionally since 2010. Its core message advocates for the end of patriarchy, highlighting how men have historically wielded their power to oppress and dominate women. The concept of toxic masculinity, where men struggle to express their emotions, is detrimental not only to them but also to society and families. What we truly need now is a shift towards a more egalitarian perspective, which is the essence of this song. I chose the title "Break the Man" because it reflects my personal journey from being a broken man to becoming a better one.

Now it's 2012, I have returned to Florida from Israel and I'm renting a room in a house that has three available rooms. One of my housemates was a young Asian girl named Melanie. At the time, Melanie was facing some challenges, and I found myself drawn to her. I genuinely cared for her well-being and recognized that she needed support. Fortunately, she managed to turn her life around, got married, and now has a lovely family, which brings me great joy.

Melanie introduced me to Kava, a drink made from the root of the exotic pepper plant native to Vanuatu in the Fiji Islands. Back in 2012, there was a Kava bar in Saint Petersburg called Bula, which at the time, was the only one of its kind in the area. Besides Kava, they also served a drink called Kratom. Kratom offers a euphoric sensation as it interacts with the brain's opioid receptors. I began frequenting this bar, and surprisingly, my craving for alcohol vanished. I hadn't intended to stop drinking; I enjoyed it. However, as I started consuming Kava, my desire for alcohol completely disappeared. Over the years, I've connected with many individuals in this community and engaged in many conversations about similar experiences.

For anyone grappling with alcoholism, consider giving kava a shot. It helped me lose my craving for alcohol. Unlike alcohol, kava won't impair you, and it does offer a sense of relaxation. In 2013, I returned to the house I had left two years prior. Felicia and I had kept in touch while I was in Israel, and upon my return to Florida, we started seeing each other again. We would go out, enjoy drinks, and have long conversations, slowly piecing things back together.

CHAPTER 9

Together again!

After a couple of months back in the house, I was in great shape, weighing around 227 pounds and feeling really good. One day, while looking out the front window, I spotted a neighbor from down the street—a real nuisance, always strutting around shirtless with tattoos, acting tough. That day, he let his dog shit on my lawn and started to walk away. I rolled down the window and called out, "You're going to clean that up!" He retorted, "Shut up! Your lawn looks shit anyway". In a flash, I tossed my glasses aside, burst through the door, and leaped over a three-foot bush like Carl Lewis. Before he knew it, I pushed him so hard he fell to the ground. I pinned him down and grabbed him by the throat, a move I was all too familiar with. He was pleading, "I'm sorry, Sir! I'm sorry!" but he was completely trapped. Felicia rushed out, trying to pull me off, but I was completely focused on this guy, ignoring everything else around me.

At last, I released him. His neck was covered in dark bruises from where I had gripped him. He dashed home like a frightened child. Just minutes later, the police arrived—specifically, the Sheriff's Department. They approached the door, but I stepped outside to greet them first. I was wearing a sleeveless shirt, and I could tell they noticed my size. They exchanged glances and seemed to wonder what to do next, as if contemplating whether to take me in. Fortunately, they were fair and let me explain my side of the story. I told them I had lived in this house for over a decade with no issues, and I offered my license for them to check my record. I explained that the guy across the street was a troublemaker who had come over to provoke me, and that's how things escalated. As it turned out, one of the deputies recognized him and remarked, "I know that guy, he's an asshole". He assured me he would document everything in a way that would close the case but advised me to avoid physical confrontations in the future. I agreed, telling him to inform the neighbor to stay away from my property, and that was the last I heard from him.

In 2014, Felicia and I having reconciled decided to remarry. So, Felicia, the kids, and I headed to City Hall for a wedding officiated by a justice of the peace. Here we were, celebrating wedding number three! I might just be setting a record here— three weddings, all to the same amazing woman. 2014 turned out to be quite an eventful year! Our marriage is better in 2014

CHAPTER 9

then it ever was before the divorce. We both recognized our failings and shortcomings and committed to working on them. We had a deeper appreciation of each other. It was like when a bone is broken. After it heals it is stronger than it was before. We count our anniversaries from 1986 without subtracting the few years we were apart. We both knew it was not over in 2011.

Just married, again!

Let me share another story with you. There was a new kava bar that opened up in 2014 called Low Tide, and it quickly became a favorite spot for us and our friends. It was fresh on the scene, being only the second kava bar in the Saint Pete area. One night, however, things took a turn. First, you need to understand the vibe of the kava community. Unlike typical bars, you won't find rowdy drunks, fights, or loud arguments here. It's a laid-back atmosphere filled with beatniks and hippies, making it a wonderfully relaxing place to unwind.

But then came that night after Halloween. Three guys walked in who clearly didn't belong; they were outsiders looking for trouble. One of them was a towering figure, around 6' 2" and weighing about 220-230 pounds, while the other two were just average-sized guys, around 5' 10" and 170 pounds. They were nothing to worry about. As my wife headed to the restroom and was returning, the big guy deliberately bumped into her, trying to knock her off balance. I didn't witness it, but Felicia came straight to me to tell me what happened. She knew exactly how I would respond. I immediately confronted the guy, getting right in his face, and asked if he had just hit my wife. He feigned ignorance, asking who she was, and I pointed her out. He seemed at a loss for words, so I took matters into my own hands, shoving him and his buddy out the door. A friend of mine who saw the whole thing remarked on my strength, saying I pushed them out like it was nothing, even with one being so big.

Then the big guy made a snarky comment, which I can't recall, but I do remember my instinct kicking in. I swung at him, landing several solid punches to the face, and by the next day, my hand was in agony from the impact. Keep in mind that my arthritis is quite severe, and these days, when I strike someone, I end up hurting myself just as much as I hurt them. However, I will not tolerate anyone laying a hand on my wife or showing her disrespect. Interestingly, in the past decade, I've been the only one to engage in a fight within the kava community. It's generally a laid-back group, and I consider myself easygoing too, but crossing the line with my wife is a different story. I had some back up nearby if things escalated, but it wrapped up quickly. Felicia actually handled one of the smaller guys. She

CHAPTER 9

pushed him and he ran out the door. He wanted no part of an angry Black woman, LOL. I landed a few solid punches, and they chose to flee. Surprisingly, I found the whole experience rather enjoyable. I did face some consequences; there was talk of banning me from the community, but ultimately, they decided against it. After all, I'm Randy, a familiar face around here, and everyone likes me. Given the situation, they felt my actions were warranted. So, I wasn't banned, but I did make a promise to refrain from any more fights. And that brings us to the end of 2014, a truly memorable and thrilling year for both me and Felicia.

I want to reintroduce a metaphor that resonates with me which I introduced in the preface. The Japanese term **Kintsugi** refers to the art of repairing broken items with gold. If you look it up, you'll find beautiful images of plates, cups, and vases that have been restored in this way. The essence of Kintsugi is that something once broken can be repaired and transformed into something even more beautiful and valuable than it was before. Unlike our culture that just throws away an item that's broken, they still see value and seek to repair rather than replace. The deeper meaning should not be overlooked. Too often we seek to replace people in our lives when times are tough, or the road gets rough. We need to value others more and things less. We don't throw people away who are damaged. We repair them.

I've mentioned before that my relationship with my children was strained. They welcomed me back, but there was a noticeable distance between us, and we were somewhat disconnected initially. It took a considerable amount of time, but eventually, we managed to rebuild our relationship. In 2015, I was diagnosed with skin cancer, specifically basal cell carcinoma. After spending years working outdoors on the

Atlantic City boardwalk, I had neglected to use sunscreen. About 30 years later and here I was facing skin cancer. I had two spots removed from my forehead and one from my right nostril, which involved significant surgery and was incredibly painful.

Now, let's jump to June 2018, a pivotal moment in my life. One night, around 2 AM on a late Friday, I woke up with the most intense abdominal pain I had ever felt. I was doubled over, struggling to breathe due to the agony. The pain eased enough after about an hour for me to carry on with my day, though I still found myself in discomfort. By the following Monday night, Felicia insisted we go to the hospital, so we headed to Largo Medical Center. I explained my situation, and they performed a CT scan. The doctor returned with alarming news: I needed to be admitted because my abdomen was filled with blood, and they needed to determine the source.

The next morning, I met with a very kind surgeon, Dr. Reynolds, with whom I would develop a close bond over the next six weeks. He proposed an exploratory surgery using a laparoscope through my navel to investigate further. The next day, during the procedure, he took one look inside and immediately decided that they needed to perform full surgery. So, they prepared me for that. Doctor Reynolds approached Felicia with a serious expression. He informed her that they needed to perform surgery on me which involved removing most of the stomach. They essentially gutted me from the bottom of my rib cage to my navel. During the procedure, they discovered not only blood but also a mass in my stomach, which fortunately turned out to be benign. However, the exterior of my stomach appeared as if it had ruptured. The presentation was so unusual that Dr Reynolds called in his partner to consult with. They had never seen anything quite like what they were seeing this day. They ended up removing 90% of my stomach, and for the first couple of days post-surgery, I felt relatively stable. The painkillers were effective, and while I experienced discomfort, it wasn't unbearable.

Then, disaster struck: I suffered an anastomosis tear. This occurred where the remaining part of my stomach was stitched to my esophagus and the connection had torn apart. The doctors believed this was due to my long-term use of Prednisone, which had weakened the tissue over the years. This complication led to severe infections throughout my body, and I struggled to breathe as one of my lungs filled with fluid. A tube was inserted into my left side to drain the fluid, and the procedure was agonizing with no anesthetic. I spent three weeks in critical care, teetering on the brink of death multiple times. There were moments when the doctor urged my wife to come quickly, fearing for my life. The doctor even considered another surgery but hesitated, worried I wouldn't survive it. Thankfully, I didn't need another operation, and after five weeks in the hospital, I began to recover. These weeks were very eventful with multiple procedures and endless tests. The pain was excruciating .It was the worst experience of my life health wise. I can remember how weak and frail I was. Going for a ten-foot walk was a big accomplishment. I had several IV lines, an NG tube, oxygen and a catheter. There were a lot of things that happened during the long hospital stay but being semi-conscious for several weeks, I don't recall all of them.

One funny incident that I do remember was one day I was really tanked up on Dilaudid, a very strong opioid, and hallucinating. I saw Earth, Wind and Fire performing before me. I was humming the song *September*. Felicia asked me what I was doing? I said, don't you see them? Earth, Wind and Fire are right there. We still laugh about that from time to time.

After spending five weeks in the hospital, primarily in critical care, I was transferred to rehab for an additional week and a half to rebuild my strength so I could stand and walk again. Being confined to a bed for so long had caused my muscles to weaken significantly, leaving me very frail. I despised the rehab sessions because I was constantly battling nausea, but I pushed through because I knew I had to. Eventually, I returned home after a long journey that began in June and concluded in August. I was shocked at my appearance. It was the first time I had seen myself in the mirror in six weeks and I was emaciated.

Just six days after arriving home, I found myself in excruciating pain, prompting a frantic trip to the emergency room. Another CT scan revealed a pulmonary embolism in my left lung and a massive blood clot in the inferior vena cava. I was quickly admitted and placed on a heparin drip. The next day, an interventional radiologist performed a procedure to remove the large clot and inserted a stent and filter. Afterward, the doctor informed me that it was one of the largest blood clots he had ever encountered, and had I not sought help, I would have most likely died. Ironically, I hadn't even gone to the hospital for the clot; I was there because of the pain. Sometimes, pain serves as a crucial warning sign.

Back at home, my recovery was painfully slow and challenging. A few months later, I developed an esophageal stricture, which meant my esophagus had narrowed significantly. While it should be about an inch wide, mine had shrunk to the size of a straw. I had been reliant on a feeding tube for months, which I absolutely loathed. Once it was removed, I attempted to eat normally, but the stricture made it impossible to swallow food. When I was first admitted in June, I weighed 225 pounds, but

CHAPTER 9

by the time I left in August, I had dropped to 185. A forty pound loss in six weeks. Due to the stricture, my weight plummeted to an astonishing 136 pounds. I looked emaciated and frail, a shadow of my former self.

I shed nearly 90 pounds, leaving me looking gaunt and on the brink of death—quite literally. If it weren't for another major surgery, I might not have made it. The nine months between my first and second surgeries were grueling; I hadn't fully healed from the first one. Seeking help, I consulted specialists at the University of South Florida in Tampa. I was battling bile reflux, which had me vomiting two to three times daily and experiencing reflux at night. The bile was damaging my esophagus, leading to a condition known as erosive esophagitis. This situation was unsustainable, as it could eventually result in esophageal cancer.

The doctor was straightforward, warning me that the upcoming surgery would be far more challenging than the first. He was absolutely right. In the months leading up to the surgery, I lost count of how many times we had to stop the car so I could vomit on the roadside. Eating out became a thing of the past, as food often got lodged in my esophagus, making it hard to breathe and increasing my risk of choking. In the two years that followed this surgery, I aspirated food so frequently that I developed pneumonia five times over two years. On one occasion, my condition worsened to the point of sepsis, with a fever of 104 and my blood oxygen plummeting to 83. I was delirious and rushed to the hospital, where my white blood cell count was alarmingly high. After a few days of intensive antibiotics and treatment, I started to recover.

In April 2019 I found myself at Tampa General Hospital. My surgeon, the chief of gastrointestinal surgeries at USF, was set to perform a total esophogogastrectomy. This procedure involved removing the esophageal stricture, what remained of my stomach, and a section of my intestines, along with another complex procedure known as Roux-en-Y.

I can't quite put into words what it all means, but I know it involved some sort of reconfiguration of my intestines, shifting things around so that what used to be higher up was now lower down, which helped reduce the bile reflux. Thankfully, the procedure was a success. However, I must say that the doctor was serious about the pain involved. The severity of pain I felt from that surgery was unlike anything I had ever encountered before, and I had already endured severe pain from my initial surgery and recovery. I was in agony in the hospital, practically screaming for more pain relief; I had never experienced such intense pain in my life. I spent two weeks in the hospital before finally going home, but the recovery was a long and painful journey.

When I finally had enough strength to venture out with my wife for some fresh air, friends who saw me were taken aback by my frail appearance. I was extremely thin, gaunt, and pale looking like a shadow of my former self. Our friends that were aware of all that had happened commented to me that I was one tough son of a bitch. It was a very hard, long battle. Now, I'm still on the road to recovery. From 2018 to 2020, I spent most of those two years in bed recuperating. Then, just as we were getting through that, COVID hit, and I found myself confined to the house for yet another year. In July 2020, we welcomed Charlie, our kitten, into our lives. He was just eight weeks old when we got him, and Felicia brought him home to keep me company. He turned out to be a wonderful companion, and I'm so grateful for his presence. He is the cutest little guy.

In August 2020, I underwent a procedure known as an anterior cervical discectomy and fusion, ACDF for short, where they performed a double fusion on my C5 and C6, as well as C6 and C7 vertebrae. I had bulging and ruptured discs, along with impinged nerves and stenosis. The excruciating pain in my left shoulder, stemming from C5, vanished after the surgery. However, I still deal with neck pain and can only move my neck in certain ways without discomfort. I must be cautious and sleep on a wedge-shaped pillow to prevent any reflux issues. Additionally, I need to maintain a gap of about three hours between my last meal and when I lie down. If I lay down earlier than that, I'm going to deal with bile reflux. I'm not sure if you have ever experienced that, but the taste of bile is just disgusting.

Charlie

By the end of 2020, with COVID in full swing, I found myself reluctant to go out. It was almost like I developed a phobia about leaving my home. I rarely attended church and preferred to stay in. This really took a toll on me, and I know it affected many others too. My personality seemed to be radically altered.

I've come to terms with my lifelong health challenges, which include difficulties with swallowing. I visit my gastroenterologist once or twice a year to have my esophagus dilated for easier swallowing. From 2018-2020 I had 16 endoscopies to stretch my esophagus so I could swallow more easily. Nutritionally, I face hurdles due to the absence of my stomach, where many essential vitamins and nutrients are absorbed. This has led to frequent vitamin deficiencies and anemia, as my body struggles to absorb nutrients effectively.

CHAPTER 9

Dental issues have also plagued me; just this year, I had two teeth break—one was crowned, and the other was extracted. The extraction took three grueling hours, during which the dentist broke the tooth and left a root behind. The pain from that procedure was excruciating and lingered for weeks, compounded by a dry socket. Fortunately, I found an orthodontist who swiftly removed the remaining root in under a minute, allowing my healing process to finally begin. One of my front teeth ended up getting chipped, a consequence of nutrient deficiency.

My weight has been stuck at around 160 pounds; I might fluctuate by a couple of pounds, but I always return to that number. It's hard to believe I was 225 pounds when this journey started. I had to completely revamp my wardrobe—once an extra-large shirt wearer, I now fit into mediums. Even my pants and underwear had to be downsized. My nuts were falling out of my undies so it was time to buy a smaller size. Energy, strength, and maintaining a proper diet are ongoing challenges for me. There are times when I forget to eat entirely due to a complete lack of appetite. While I've found some stability, lingering issues remain.

When I was hospitalized in 2018, I had already been prescribed opioids for my neck, back pain, and arthritis. The biologic treatments for my psoriatic arthritis didn't work, leading to a prescription for oxycodone. I managed to use them sparingly at first, but after six weeks in the hospital on high doses of morphine and other opioids, I found myself addicted. For the next two to three years, I relied on these medications to cope with the pain during my recovery.

Eventually, I no longer needed them, but the addiction persisted. I spent the following two years grappling with opioid addiction. Once I recognized that I was abusing the medication, I realized I was taking more than prescribed. A 30-day prescription would often run out two or three days early, and at times, I would find myself waiting five to seven days for a refill. There was even a month where I endured a grueling ten-day wait. The withdrawal was pure torment—sweating, diarrhea, cramps, and nausea made those days feel like hell. Being Dope Sick is no fun.

I remember asking for help during those dark days. I turned to my wife for support in this situation. I had purchased a small lock box where she would store the pills, taking the key with her to work. However, I ended up breaking into that lock box, which didn't sit well with her. Eventually, I reached a breaking point and asked myself why I was putting myself through this cycle month after month. I decided it was time to stop, and I quit cold turkey. I can procrastinate on many things, but once I make up my mind, there's no turning back. I've done it with cigarettes, alcohol, and gambling, and now, a year later, I haven't touched an opioid. I don't think about them or crave them.

I still deal with abdominal pain from scar tissue and adhesions, along with joint pain from osteo and psoriatic arthritis. But isn't that just part of life? We all face our own battles. The real question is how we choose to respond. Will we let bitterness and anger consume us, or will we accept our struggles with humility? We can either improve our situation or let it drag us down. The choice is ours. I've learned that when we humble ourselves, we receive grace to endure and overcome. Complaining and resisting only keeps us stuck in the mess. Yes, there's divine providence, but we must also face the consequences of our choices in certain circumstances. If we surrender everything to God, He can transform our chaos into something wonderful. He truly has the power to do that.

You might be familiar with opioids and painkillers, but my struggle went beyond just alleviating physical discomfort. I was attempting to numb the emotional turmoil that had weighed me down for years. Countless individuals around us are grappling with various forms of pain—emotional, spiritual, and physical—seeking solace in substances like drugs, alcohol, or fleeting pleasures to escape their suffering. After a long journey, I learned a crucial lesson: you can run from your pain, but you can never truly hide from it. The path to healing requires confronting your inner demons and acknowledging your hurt. The more you try to ignore or suppress it, the longer your healing will be delayed. I'll revisit this topic later.

On a brighter note, something positive did come out of 2020. After returning from Israel in 2012, I was still grappling with atheism. I had mentioned before how I struggled to reconcile a sovereign God with the evil I witnessed in the world. Then I met a friend named Joe Gallucio, who became a close confidant. Joe was incredibly patient; we would discuss atheism, and he, being a Deacon in the Orthodox Church, would listen and share insights. Gradually, I began to realize that I did believe in God; I just couldn't figure out how to align that belief with the existence of evil. Over time, I learned to reconcile these ideas. People have free will. When someone chooses to drink excessively and then drives, resulting in the death of an innocent person, that individual is accountable for their actions. God didn't go to the bar, get drunk, or drive that car. That's the reality of our world. God has granted us free will and choices.

Eventually, I decided to return to the Catholic Church but Joe and I continued to talk about religion. I wasn't ready to embrace Orthodoxy yet, but after about a year, I found myself struggling with the modernism prevalent in Catholicism. There was a lot of modernism creeping into Evangelicalism too, turning it into a circus, a clown show. Where was the reverence? Where was the awe for God? What was happening? I had been delving into the study of Orthodoxy, immersing myself in literature and uncovering its essence. It became clear to me that Orthodoxy represents the culmination and continuation of Judaism, embodying true Messianic Judaism. Jesus and Paul were not seeking to establish a new faith; they were Jews through and through, with Jesus being the foretold Jewish Messiah. In the book of Revelation, Jesus is called The Lion of the Tribe of Judah. Jesus never losses his Jewish identity. He is called the Son of David several times in the New Testament. My perspective has shifted significantly because of this exploration.

One key insight I gained is that the worship practices of the Jews in the temple were divinely ordained, not merely human inventions. God provided specific instructions on how He was to be worshiped. Transitioning to the New Testament, it's evident that early Christianity was a natural extension of Judaism. This is echoed in the book of Hebrews and the letters of Saint Paul, who emphasizes that there is a proper way to conduct oneself in the House of God, a way to worship Him with reverence and awe. If there is a prescribed method, it implies that not every approach is valid. I discovered that worship is not a free-for-all; it cannot be improvised on a whim, or changed to reflect the modern culture. Worship is directed towards God. He is the audience. Yet, what I observe in contemporary Christianity, both in Catholic and Evangelical settings, often includes smoke machines, light displays, rock music, and even clowns. This reflects a clash between post-Enlightenment

CHAPTER 9

thinking, fundamentalism, and a more permissive attitude that seems to dominate today.

On one hand, there was rigid fundamentalism and narrow-mindedness, while on the other, an anything-goes mentality. Neither of these extremes resonated with me. My religious beliefs were evolving, and I sensed that more changes were on the horizon. I stumbled upon Orthodoxy, which I believe represents the early church and the truest form of Christianity. Latin Catholicism emerged later, followed by Protestantism even further down the line. As I delved into the writings of the early church fathers, I found myself captivated; their teachings were a stark contrast to what I had recently encountered in both Protestant and Catholic circles. I realized that those who knew and were taught by the Apostles were in the best position to know exactly what Jesus and his Apostles believed and what the early church practiced. I see now that when I was an Evangelical we followed the Reformers and those who came after them as if the first fifteen centuries of the church never existed.

By way of clarification, while I disagree with much of modern Western Christianity, both Catholic and Protestant, I have no doubt that many in both communions are true believers. I have had conversations with many in those churches that express the same concerns over Modernism that I do. Their reasons for remaining within those churches are their own and I do not judge them or their decisions. We all believe we are following the Truth or we wouldn't be where we are. We would be somewhere else. I thought I was right many times in the past only to change my mind and embrace something else later. I have to remain humble. I simply remember I am a Jew who was baptized Catholic, then embraced Evangelicalism only to return to Catholicism for a season.

This exploration led to a profound conversion for me—one to Eastern Orthodoxy, culminating in my baptism in 2020. Joe became my godfather and has been a trusted friend for many years now. The perspectives I will share shortly have garnered mixed reactions within the church; some embrace my beliefs, while others do not. Every religion has its share of fundamentalists and exclusivists, but I no longer align with either.

I still consider myself an Orthodox Christian, however I self-identify as a Jew who believes that Jesus is the promised Messiah revealed by the Jewish prophets of the Tanach (What Jews call their bible and what Christians call the Old Testament). Most Christians are Gentiles who believe in Christ. Believers were first called "Christians" in Antioch, a Gentile city. The earliest disciples and all the apostles were Jews who had found the Messiah of Israel. I balk over the word Christ at times because it is Greek in origin, but it does transliterate Messiah from the Hebrew and the New Testament was written in Greek. My issue is that using Christ in place of Messiah removes the Jewishness of Jesus and minimizes the role of the Jewish people in the history of salvation. After all Jesus said that "Salvation is from the Jews" John 4:22. It reinforces that separation between Judaism and early Christianity that only developed decades after the beginnings of the Jesus movement; early church.

I believe in the teaching of the Eastern Orthodox church. The Trinity, the Sacraments and The Blessed Virgin Mary, etc. However it's important to note that these days I temper my convictions with the knowledge that I have been wrong before and need to maintain a level of humility when it comes to things that can be beyond our understanding. Previously I held tenaciously to the conviction that my particular understanding of theology was correct, only to change my mind later.

I read a meme on Facebook by an Orthodox saint that said, the whole Gospel is summed up in compassion. But I just read a meme by the Dalai Lama that said Compassion is the essence of Buddhism. Then it hit me. Now bear with me as I quote a few bible verses. Relax you might be pleasantly surprised with what I present. First, in the gospel of John Chapter One it says that Jesus is the True light that enlightens every person coming into the world. St Paul says that the grace of God that brings salvation has appeared to all people. St Paul also says that God is the Savior of ALL people. Then the thought hit me. You mean that everyone who walks this life following the path of compassion, kindness and mercy are doing so because they have Seen the Light and have experienced the grace of God, whether they know the source or not?

You see I no longer believe that only those who possess a proper intellectual understanding of the Christian Gospel are Saved i.e. going to be with God in eternity. We are united to God by faith NOT intellect, knowledge, or doctrines. The bible says that he that comes to God must believe that he is. It doesn't say you cannot come unless you have this particular knowledge of these certain truths. I believe that Orthodoxy is the fullness of the faith. The full revelation of the saving truth of the Gospel. But where does it say you must have the fullness, you must have it all to be accepted by God? Nowhere. So, what I now believe is that all who by God's grace whether they know it or not who follow the path of love, peace, mercy, kindness and compassion are following the true God. Whether they know it or not. I know this is heresy to some. I get it. Burn me. Our good deeds are the fruit of a good heart. When the bible speaks of the Final Judgment, people are not judged on their theological knowledge. There is no bible quiz. They are judged based on how they treated their fellow humans.

I used to be a narrow-minded Pharisee myself. Every religion has its fundamentalists. They think they and only they have the truth and everything else is false. I'm not sure what attracts people to Fundamentalism, but I suspect it is the comfort they feel when they don't have to think for themselves or seek the truth. Someone else does all the work. They take comfort being in their little box. They are shielded from the world outside and congregate with only those who think as they do. People take comfort in being insulated as well as isolated from those they deem as Others or Outsiders. I suppose that we are all very tribal by nature and seek to be among those who are most like us, be it ethnically, religiously or politically. What I have also observed about fundamentalists in general regardless of the particular religion they belong to is that they can become very mean spirited, critical and judgmental of everything that does not conform to their narrow view. People often become political fundamentalists without even realizing it. If you demonize those who have a different view than yourself, you are probably a fundamentalist. I have found that when we put our preconceived ideas of other people aside and actually talk to them, we have more in common than not. The remaining small areas of disagreement we can negotiate or set aside.

I am not a Universalist who believes that everyone will enjoy God in eternity. Why? Because some don't want to have anything to do with God now and God will allow them their free will, free choice into eternity. God doesn't force anyone to love him. I realize that I could be completely wrong but this is my current thinking. Now my understanding differs a lot from the Western Christian tradition that sees Heaven and Hell

CHAPTER 9

as locations. I am aware that the bible speaks of the Father in heaven, while his Spirit is everywhere. As this book is primarily a memoir and not a theological work, I've chosen to keep those details to a minimum. The Eastern Christian tradition is very different. We start from the position that God is Everywhere. Psalm 139:7-12 expresses the truth that you cannot escape the presence of God. Ecclesiastes 12:7 says that at physical death the body returns to the dust from which it came, and the spirit returns to God who gave it. The implication is that all return to God.

In the Eastern Orthodox view, the only question is how each individual will experience the presence of God. Will it be heaven or hell? God never changes. Only we change. Our disposition towards God is the determining factor as to how we will experience God. The example I give when discussing heaven, I say, if you hate God now, the presence of God will be hell to you. Just think how you feel when you must spend time with someone you really can't stand. Every second is torture. You hate being in that person's presence. So, God allows each of us the freedom to choose our own destiny. But if you love God now it will be like being in the company of a friend where the time just flies, and you love every second. That's how I see it anyway. I don't speak for any church; I just speak for myself.

I am not an exclusivist either. I was when I was an Evangelical. We were told endlessly that Jesus is the way, the truth and the life. No one comes to the Father except through him. In their understanding that meant you must possess explicit knowledge in order to experience the favorable presence of God in eternity. But where does the verse say that? It doesn't. Yes, I believe that Jesus is the Savior, the Messiah. He is the only true way but where does the verse say that you must possess all the explicit knowledge and information about him to be with God eternally? I don't see it that way anymore. Do I have to understand how electricity works for me to benefit from it or can I just flick a switch and turn the lights on?

What I see is that those who follow the path of compassion and mercy are doing so because they have experienced the Grace of God that brings salvation. They have been enlightened by the True Light that enlightens every person coming into the world. The Protestant church is steeped in Post Enlightenment thinking and may not even realize it. Reason and Logic guide them and there is no place for mystery. They talk about the metaphysical but have no place for it in their understanding of God. The prophet Isaiah says that *"God's ways are not our ways, and his thoughts are not our thoughts"* Isaiah 55:8. Intellect and reason will lead you to a cerebral knowledge of theology with the possibility of not experiencing the Divine. I can say with all confidence that if you speak of God with mathematical certainty and precision, you are NOT speaking of God. You are speaking of an entity that you have created in your own image. You can have a head full of knowledge with an empty soul. We can know what God has revealed but beyond that there is much more that we don't know than what we do know. God is mysterious and other worldly.

A final word about the unchanging nature of God. Throughout scripture we are called to turn back to God, to return to Him. "Draw near to God and He will draw near to you" James 4:8. God never changes, and He is always there. We have moved away from Him and like the father in the story of the Prodigal Son (Luke 15) He is awaiting our return to Him. When God warned Adam and Eve that they would die upon eating from the Tree of the knowledge of good and evil (Genesis 2:17), He NEVER said

CHAPTER 9

He would KILL them. He said they would die. Why? Because they choose to live life apart from and separated from the only One who is Life, Light and Love. That is what spiritual death is. A separation from God. When Jesus said, I am come that you may have life, he was speaking to people who were alive physically. But there is more than just this physical existence. We can enter into the life of God and be one with Him. God has no need to change, we do. He is always there waiting for us to return to Him.

May I say an additional word on those who disbelieve. There are many who have had a bad experience at the hands of people who have claimed to represent God. Some of these people are wicked and evil and have caused innocent souls much pain and suffering. As a result, many have abandoned Christianity or whatever belief they held to. I am not so sure that God will reject these souls. God is love and sees all. He understands us better than we understand ourselves. I see it as people rejecting not God but those who claimed to represent him. God takes all mitigating circumstances into consideration. Rather than condemning these souls, he may wipe every tear from their faces and welcome them as a loving father. It is not for me to judge who is accepted by God. I only present this as a possibility that I happen to believe in. I view everything from the starting point of God's love.

Now I see that we need to follow the Light we have been given. Experience the grace that has appeared to us, and live the life of love. Start loving people and when you do that whatever knowledge you need will be easily revealed to you in God's time. Stop thinking so hard about what the Truth is. There was a Catholic theologian years ago named Karl Rahner who in the 20th century introduced a teaching about what he called

"The Anonymous Christian." By this he meant people who don't identify as Christians but are because they are following the Light of the World (Jesus) whether they realize it or not. I don't know how his view differs from my own, but it does sound similar. He was considered a heretic by some and a revolutionary by others. I no longer use labels as a litmus test to see who is a fellow believer. There are many false brethren out there and the bible warns us about them often. I have known too many people who described themselves as Christians but lived and acted like devils. I don't care what you call yourself. How you treat others is what matters. The bible even says, show me your faith by your works. Love is the fulfillment of the law. If you follow the path of love, you will never stumble. I will refer you back to my comments about the Final Judgment being according to our works of charity and not our knowledge.

To me it's impossible for a person to live a life of sacrifice and service to others apart from God dwelling in that person's soul whether they are aware of it or not. Who am I to condemn the Buddhist who is kind and compassionate yet lacks an intellectual understanding of the teachings of Jesus? To me it's more important to do the teachings of Jesus in how you live your life. Showing compassion, offering assistance to those in need, this is what Jesus teaches his disciples. Those who do such things belong to God and are following the Light that has been given to them. I would rather be a loving atheist or Buddhist on Judgment day than an unforgiving, hate filled Christian.

The church is filled with Pharisees. Those with a very narrow view of things. I was one myself years ago. I was taught to be one. I have discovered that God is bigger than the church and can be found by all people who desire Him. After all everything in creation belongs to Him. Those who follow this path I've laid

CHAPTER 9

out when they leave this life and enter eternity will see the True and Living God and say, "Oh it's you." God will receive them into heaven i.e. his favorable presence. These are my beliefs. I am not an evangelist and am not trying to convert you to my belief system, I'm only sharing what it is.

Let me say a word about Atheists and those who reject religion, as I have experienced this myself. It's important to examine why a person is rejecting religion as I've discussed earlier. Of course, there are those who believe Science has disproved the existence of God. Then there are those who are like I was for a few years. We cannot reconcile the idea of an all-powerful good God with the evil that is rampant in this world. I get it. I have been there. Then there is another kind of Atheist. That is the person who does not like the idea of a Higher Authority proclaiming that their immorality is wrong and harmful. They want to live life on their own terms regardless of consequences. I understand that. I have been there too.

But as I have grown older, I have come to see and understand that whatever God prohibits is for our good. Whatever he forbids is to spare us from pain and sorrow. I have just recently come to hold firmly to this understanding myself. But there is a larger community that have rejected God and religion because of their personal experiences. For example, if someone was abused by a father or father figure as a child, it will be very difficult if not impossible for this individual to put their trust in a God who claims to be a loving father. It's perfectly understandable. Do you think that God doesn't understand this? Do you think that He doesn't have compassion for this person? Here's what I believe about such situations and similar ones where a person has been damaged, and their understanding of God has been skewed by the behavior of others. God not only has compassion but weeps at the damage done to this individual. Just as Jesus wept at the tomb of his friend Lazarus when he died. Jesus not only missed his friend but was overcome with emotion seeing Lazarus's sisters weeping over the loss of their brother.

The bible tells us to rejoice with those who rejoice and weep with those who weep. What makes you think God does any less? For those who insist that those who don't express explicit faith in God are doomed to an eternity in hell, here's what I believe is closer to the truth. God will see that this innocent soul has gone through hell through no fault of their own. When they die, I believe God will wipe away every tear from their eyes. God is love and love keeps no record of wrongs.

There is another group that has an issue with God. They are mad at him and blame him for all their troubles. There are those who have lost children. The most terrible thing that a human being can experience has to be the loss of a child. I can only sincerely offer them my compassion and concern. But we must keep in mind that God has given us as those created in his image Free Will. Much of what happens in the world is the result of our poor choices. Sometimes we do not know why something has happened. But there are times when we do. For example, when a drunk driver kills an innocent human being. May I remind you that God did not go to that bar and order too many drinks and then get behind the wheel drunk. No, the responsibility falls on the person who did the drinking and made a horrible decision to drive drunk.

Sometimes a child dies from drugs. We see too much of this awful thing in our society recently. But no one wants to investigate what drove this person to drugs? There are parents who would rather blame God for not intervening than look in

CHAPTER 9

the mirror and ask themselves the hard questions. Have I failed my child? What mistakes have I made when they were young that may have contributed to this destructive behavior? Hard questions I know. But, until we are willing to ask ourselves these hard questions, we will continue to sit in the pile of shit we have had out of our lives. I know it hurts. I know it is not easy. But it is necessary to move past these problems and to begin the healing. The only way to be cured of cancer is to remove it. As long as it is within you, you will remain sick. Sometimes in body and soul. This is not what God desires for any of us. Stop listening to the Devil. He is a liar. God wants to heal you and make you whole. Are you not sick and tired of being sick and tired? The choice is yours. He gives us Free Will.

Another example of hard talk happened a few months ago. I was visiting Kay, my favorite kava tender at the Kava bar I frequent. She was having a conversation with a young man who was distraught after his girlfriend had broken up with him because of his continued drug use. Kay was trying to offer words of consolation to make him feel better. They were both within three feet of me and I could hear every word. There was no attempt at making this a private conversation so I wasn't eavesdropping. After about ten minutes, the young man turned to me and said, what do you think I should do? I never offer advice or an opinion unless I am asked first. He asked so I told him. I said, I'm going to speak to you like a man okay? He said, yes please do. I told him, it's your fault the girl left you and only you can create the conditions for your reconciliation somewhere down the line. I told him a woman wants to be protected, not hurt. She is protecting her heart and doesn't want to be hurt by you again. She can't trust you right now. What you need to do now is work on yourself and your addiction.

You have to do it for yourself, not for her or to get her back. In the future if she sees that she can trust you with her heart, you might have a chance at a future together. These were not easy words to hear but they were true. He teared up a bit and realized that I was right and thanked me.

The Bible says, *"Faithful are the wounds of a friend. Deceitful are the kisses of an enemy."* If you don't have a friend that will be truthful with you, you better go find one. Thankfully I have several. It hurts to hear the truth at times, but like medicine, it is good for you.

A final word about religion and belief. I have many friends that believe in "manifesting to the Universe." I appreciate that they acknowledge there is something bigger than themselves and beyond us. BUT the Universe is not a person. The Universe has no feelings or concern about individuals. God is a person. He is the Almighty Creator. He can hear our prayers and cries. I present this for your consideration if you too are "manifesting to the Universe." Again, I'm glad you recognize there is something out there, but that 'something' is personal. God is a Person and you are created to be his image bearer.

Chapter 10

Sowing the Seeds of Love

I've titled this chapter "Sowing the Seeds of Love," inspired by the song from Tears for Fears. This title truly encapsulates my evolving perspective on faith, humanity, and the expectations that God has for us. I believe it resonates even with those who may not identify with a particular faith but strive to be good individuals. We are all called to cultivate love in our lives. As I survey 2024, I feel like everything has finally fallen into place for me. Over the past year, God has been working on me, peeling back layers like an onion, addressing various emotional struggles, traumas, and experiences one by one. This journey has humbled me and left me feeling broken at times. I found myself in tears, mourning, and reaching out for help. It was exactly what I needed.

 A dear friend whom I mentioned earlier, Arin, introduced me to a film titled *"A Monster Calls."* It's challenging to put into words if you haven't seen it, but it beautifully explores the healing process of emotional trauma. If you haven't seen it yet, I highly recommend it; you might need to view it a few times to fully grasp its depth. I know I did. There is a video on

YouTube that discusses the movie from a psychological point of view. It features a therapist and a film maker who really break down what is happening. I highly recommend it. The channel is Cinema Therapy.

God had been dealing with me for some time and the layers of armor were being pulled back and stripped away. I was changing. I was healing. I am sure that my health challenges that began in earnest in 2018 were part of the healing process. I had to be broken first. You cannot be healed until you admit you are sick, and even then you must desire it. I lived the life of a fake for decades. Smiling, laughing and making everyone think I was fine. I wasn't. I was broken with poison running through my veins. Without meaning to, I was causing pain to everyone around me. Hurt people, hurt people.

Arin played a pivotal role in helping me understand that salvation encompasses every aspect of our being. It's not merely about the forgiveness of sins or the promise of an afterlife, as we often focused on in Protestantism. Instead, it begins in the present, focusing on the healing process that allows us to return to our original design as bearers of God's image—reflecting His nature. We are spirit, soul and body. If any part is wounded or sick it will effect the rest. Western civilization has been so preoccupied with materialism that we have neglected our souls. That immaterial part of ourselves that are just as real as our physical bodies. Many are awakening to this deficiency in our society and lives. The Spirituality section of bookstores are growing larger and larger all the time. People are hungry. But when people are starving they will eat anything. There is a darkness that we need to be aware of and guard against. Evil is real and so are evil spirits. I only mention this to encourage you to exercise discernment. Satan can disguise

CHAPTER 10

himself as an angel of Light and he is the Father of lies. But as the saying goes, the truth *is* out there.

A few months back, I received a diagnosis of PTSD stemming from past traumas and the relentless pain I endured from surgeries, which had profoundly changed me. I consulted a psychiatrist who prescribed Klonopin, starting with half a milligram twice daily for three weeks. I felt increasingly weak but failed to connect this with my long-standing Myasthenia Gravis condition. By the fourth week, my dosage was increased to one milligram twice a day, and just six days later, I found myself unable to walk or stand without assistance, experiencing a severe flare-up of Myasthenia Gravis.

This condition can be life-threatening, particularly because it impacts breathing and my lung capacity was diminished upon examination. My wife rushed me to the emergency room, where a neurologist inquired about any new medications. It hit me then—FUCK, how could I have overlooked that! ASSUME NOTHING. My aunt who's a nurse said to me that I should have double checked the medication before taking it. I usually take great care to monitor my medications. I reminded her that I wasn't the one who went to school for twelve years to become a doctor and he was the one who should have done that. We discontinued the Klonopin immediately, and I was treated with high doses of steroids and admitted to the hospital for IVIG therapy. This blood product works by flooding the body with beneficial antibodies to combat the harmful ones. The next day, I felt a significant improvement thanks to the steroids and IVIG, and all I could think about was getting home. I have a deep aversion to hospitals, haunted by past experiences that left me with nightmares.

While I'm in the hospital trying to recover, I received a harsh message from my sister through Facebook Messenger. It's important to note that my sister and mother chose to cut ties with me many years ago. Despite my attempts to mend our relationship, they wanted nothing to do with me. Eventually they decided to see me when I made a trip to New Haven after a twenty year period of estrangement. I was the one who initiated the reconciliation. We met but there was still tension. They've never met my children or even inquired about their names. I had buried so much pain that I struggled to recall every hurtful thing they had done to me but my wife and daughter remembered. My sister had been particularly unkind to both my wife and daughter when I left for Israel, but I won't delve into those details as they don't serve the story. However, her recent message was the final straw; she accused me of not caring about our mother and being profoundly selfish. If I cared at all, I would have visited her, even though it had been nearly a decade since I last saw her.

My sister fails to grasp the nature of my medical issues, which fluctuate not just daily but sometimes hourly. As of the time of this writing I have been hospitalized twice for bowel obstructions. Due to the nature of my anatomy, and the abdominal adhesions I have because of the surgeries, this is a common complication. I have anxiety about traveling knowing this condition can cause me to be rushed to the hospital at anytime.

Setting my mother and sister aside for a moment, I have dear friends in that area—friends I've known for nearly 50 years. I would love to visit them, regardless of whether my mother and sister were there. My sister attempted to manipulate my feelings, insisting I should come see our mother. She learned well from my mother.

CHAPTER 10

She claimed our mother suffers from Alzheimer's and intimated that she is providing round-the-clock care and covering all her expenses. When I first read her message, it shattered me. I was in the hospital with my daughter by my side, and I couldn't help but cry. The pain from my sister's words reopened old wounds. Wounds that would finally be healed after fifty years. I had come to the end of the road. It was time to face the demon. I found myself in tears. The pain was overwhelming, but my sister's actions had unearthed a deep-seated wound I had kept hidden for many years. While her intention was to hurt me, she inadvertently did me a tremendous favor. It allowed me to finally express everything I had bottled up inside—talking, shouting, crying—facing my emotions head-on like never before. I was remembering things that had been long hidden and buried. I believe that everything I had experienced earlier this year was leading me to this moment, peeling back layers of my past. Perhaps this was the final layer.

I reflected on my sister's harsh words, particularly regarding my mother. Contrary to her claims, my mother does not have Alzheimer's. How can I be so sure? I spoke with her two to three times a week, often in the mornings and sometimes in the afternoons when I pick my wife up from work. Each time I call, my mother recognizes me immediately and inquires about my wife by name. She knows exactly who we are, which doesn't align with the behavior of someone suffering from Alzheimer's. And regarding the need for 24-hour care, I've been consistently calling her for years, two to three times a week. In the past five years, there's only been one occasion when I called my mother, and she responded, "Can I call you back? Your sister is here, and I'm spending time with her." What does that imply? It suggests that every time I reach out, my sister is conveniently absent. Regarding expenses, if my mother is truly as unwell as she claims, why isn't she in an assisted living facility? At 87, she's living in a 55-and-older apartment complex, which was my sister's choice, not mine. I also noticed my sister's recent vacation photos in Tennessee with her daughter and granddaughter on Facebook. While I have no issue with her taking a break, it's ironic that she tries to guilt me for not being present while she's off enjoying herself. She even accused me of exaggerating my own health issues. Ultimately, if my mother has Alzheimer's as severely as my sister insists, what difference would my visit make? She wouldn't know who I was.

This book was released in September 2024. Since then a significant event took place. January 3rd 2025 a friend from New Haven contacted me on Facebook to offer condolences for my mother's passing. I didn't know she had died. I immediately started searching for obituaries to no avail. There was nothing. After a week I decided to call the county coroner's office to see if they had any information. After I confirmed some information she informed me that my mother died October 14th 2024. My sister told no one! Regardless of how she feels about me, a son deserves to know his mother died. She didn't even tell my uncle, my mother's brother. I'll let you draw your own conclusions about my sister's character. If anyone thought I was exaggerating about my family this should settle all doubt. My mother decided to stop speaking to me again last July due to a beef I had with my sister. She never asked me my side of the story. Never asked what happened between you and your sister? My mother went to her grave not speaking to her mother, her brother or her son. How incredibly sad it all is.

All the buried emotions from years past resurfaced, and I found myself crying and releasing all that pent-up pain. My sister's intentions may have been harmful, but in the end, it brought me healing. What seems like a curse can turn into a blessing. I confronted the demons that had haunted me for so long, unlocking memories I had kept hidden. When I was younger and single I drowned my pain in drugs, alcohol and women. In recent years suppressed my feelings, finding refuge in theology and intellectual pursuits—books upon books, devoid of emotion.

I have become a lone wolf that has found it difficult to develop truly meaningful healthy relationships. I have always had trust issues and have a highly suspicious nature. In recent years, that has changed to some degree as I have several very close male friends. Kenny Appel and I have maintained our friendship since the '70s. We have seen each other at our best and worst. Arin has also seen me at my worst and still loved me. I am grateful for these men. My childhood friends such as Jay, John and Alex are also there if I need them. Some bonds cannot be broken.

Jay, myself and Alex

I arrived home from the hospital and the next day I still feel weak, though not as severely as before. For weeks, I've been battling this weakness, trying to regain my strength. The week following my discharge from the hospital was transformative; my wife and I connected in a way we hadn't in years. I opened up to her about things she had never known. I reached out to my uncle in California, and we exchanged stories. We reminisced about those past robberies, including the ones my mother had claimed I was involved in. I was shocked to learn that my mother told the police I was responsible for the first robbery. Given my shy and timid nature as a child, the thought of me orchestrating a home robbery seemed absurd. I was less than twelve at the time.

Felicia and I found joy in each other's company again, laughing and being playful like we hadn't in ages. I shed many tears that week, but they were cathartic—tears that healed. I finally confronted my inner demons. The light dispelled the darkness, and almost overnight, I began to understand my aversion to certain things from my past. I had always been uncomfortable around strong women, having only witnessed a powerful, unstable woman in my mother, who wielded her strength to harm men. I still believe that women who harbor animosity towards men can misuse their power and seek to punish them, while those who love men can lead effectively, and I am now open to following such women. Not all women in authority despise men; for instance, the Prime Minister of Israel Golda Meyer was a remarkable leader, beloved by many.

On the flip side, I recognize that chauvinistic men often exploit their authority to dominate women, particularly in Western cultures steeped in patriarchy. This is just as harmful as the actions of women who hate men. We don't need a patriarchal or matriarchal society; God created Adam and Eve to rule together in harmony. An egalitarian society, where both genders share power for the benefit of all, may be what we need now. Both genders bring unique gifts, perspectives and attributes to the table. Perhaps it's time to break the cycle and embrace change, as highlighted in the song "Break the Man," which speaks to this very issue. We were meant to complement each other in a society where both sexes share power for the greater good.

There was a time when I really disliked the sight of a woman with a bald head or very short hair. Seems silly now. Why was that? For a few reasons. Firstly, it just didn't look natural to me. It felt akin to seeing a green steak—something just didn't look right about it. Typically, women are associated with longer hair, and most prefer it that way. But for me, it also felt like a bold statement. In many instances, it conveyed a sense of power, though not always. Because strong women such as my mother used their power to hurt men, I came to resent strong women. Even just the appearance of a strong woman turned me off. I was very critical and judgmental I know. But I'm sharing with you how my attitudes were formed. While I am an advocate for an egalitarian society, just because a woman can do anything a man can do doesn't necessarily mean she should. One example is mothers who become soldiers and leave their very young children behind to go off to war. Babies need their mothers. Young children grow stronger emotionally with a mother to support their growth. I know some will disagree with me and that's okay. Remember I have strong Egalitarian and Libertarian leanings on social issues but there are a few instances where I still believe women and men are better suited to certain activities.

Over time, I learned to temper my judgments and embrace acceptance, recognizing people for who they truly are before forming opinions about their backgrounds or choices. Appearances can be deceiving and may not reveal the intent of the heart at all. I was raised at a time when men with long hair was frowned upon. I adopted the attitudes of those whom I trusted the most and those who were most influential to me, my father and grandfather. The way I was raised, there was no liberty to be a free thinker. I was told, sit and listen. Now that I am in my Sixties, I am starting to adopt the attitudes of the so-called Hippies of the '60s. I no longer care about the length of a mans hair. I haven't for a long long time. In many cultures, it's shameful for a man to cut his hair. Since when did mid Twentieth century American culture become the standard to judge all others? In Christian fundamentalist circles, having

CHAPTER 10

long hair is akin to being in rebellion against God and a mortal sin. How silly. I've become very anti-establishment and have a distrust of those in power, especially the government. Power corrupts and absolute power corrupts absolutely. Many of these politicians are addicted to power. They are multi-millionaires in need of nothing financially. So why are they not home enjoying their grandchildren and golden years in retirement? They find power so intoxicating that they cannot leave.

This final phase of the transformation began around July 4th, Independence Day, a time when I felt I was discovering my own independence and freedom. It was a significant turning point for me. I found a renewed balance with God and those around me. My relationship with my wife flourished like never before. The narrow-minded, critical version of myself faded away, replaced by a happier man who viewed life through a new perspective.

Over the last ten years being exposed to so many Gays and Lesbians in the Kava community, my attitudes started to slowly change. Shortly after this realization that I was not the same man, I gathered my children to share my journey with them. I didn't want them to perceive me the way I had viewed my own father, a stranger in many ways. My departure from their mother and then going to Israel had caused them deep pain, and while I had slowly rebuilt their trust, a barrier remained, especially with my son. I recognized that I had mirrored my father's distance, sharing little with him. I felt compelled to confess and share my story, hoping it would help them understand me better and mend our relationship. My children knew that I had a difficult childhood, but they didn't know any details. I wasn't trying to seek absolution for my sins and failures, I just wanted them to know why I was the way I was. I didn't want them to have the same questions about me that I have about my father.

My family—my true family—means everything to me, especially those who stood by me during my darkest moments. I've completely distanced myself from my sister now. As the song "Shout" goes, *"shout, shout, let it all out—these are the things I can do without."* Trust me when I say, you don't need anyone's approval to remove anything or anyone from your life that hinders your growth, peace and well being.

This isn't the path I envisioned for myself, yet it's the one I had to take. You owe nothing to anyone but your children. They are your responsibility because you chose to bring them into this world.

I previously mentioned that in 1987, I experienced a rebirth, becoming a new person filled with love, joy, peace, and hope. Another point about my initial conversion in 1987 is that it was not mediated by any church or priest. God met me where I was. How I went from such a beautiful experience to becoming a narrow minded Fundamentalist is beyond me. I am glad He rescued me again. This time from my own erroneous beliefs. *"Reason gonna bind you, cripple and confine you."*

I learned to be narrow-minded, to view others as different and somehow unacceptable in the eyes of God. But my perspective has shifted. The Bible encourages us to seek peace and actively pursue it. That's my focus now reconciling with others when I can, confronting my inner struggles, facing my past, and striving for a brighter future. It seems that until we're ready to confront our wounds and let go of the pain, we will, as I mentioned earlier, continue to sit in the pile of shit that we have made of our lives.

So, where do I now stand spiritually? Let me share a few

insights. Recently, while listening to Foreigner's song "*I Want to Know What Love Is*," I had a revelation. As a Protestant, I had been conditioned to believe in the false dichotomy of sacred versus secular. That notion is misguided and a man made construct. There's no true separation between the two. Many think sacred refers only to hymns, church buildings, and religious practices, while anything else, like rock music, is deemed secular. But as I listened to that song, I realized that everything could hold spiritual significance. While the idea of sacred versus secular is flawed, I do believe in the concepts of holy and unholy. Making love in a healthy relationship is sacred, while violating someone is deeply wrong. Goodness can be twisted into something ugly and unholy. Listening to that song brought God to my mind, and I found myself crying out, "I want to know what love is. Please show me." You see, anything can be made holy. It all depends on your heart and where you stand. When your heart is filled with love, peace, mercy, and compassion, everything resonates differently. The bible says that, to the pure all things are pure. Who cannot relate to the line, "*In my life there's been heartache and pain. I don't know if I can take it again. Can't stop now. I've traveled too far, to change this lonely life.*"?

Are you serious? That's spiritual, at least for me. A song from the '70s that stands out from my teenage years is "Love Is the Answer" by England Dan and John Ford Coley. If you haven't heard it, you should check it out on YouTube. It's one of the most beautiful and uplifting songs I've ever encountered. One of the lines goes, "*Light of the world, shine on me, Love is the answer. Shine on us all, Set us free, Love is the Answer.*" That song shifted my perspective entirely. Suddenly, the music resonated with me in a new way, and the lyrics struck a chord deep within. Movies took on new layers of meaning, and I found myself connecting with the emotions of the characters like never before. I was becoming more empathetic, allowing myself to feel emotions I had suppressed for nearly five decades. After enduring so much pain, I had built a protective wall around myself. While I felt safe, I was also hollow—a mere shadow of who I could be. I needed to be shattered. God broke me multiple times through illness, and He kept doing so until I finally embraced my pain. I faced it head-on, and He was right there beside me. He'll be there for you too.

The Bible tells us that God is love, and I wholeheartedly believe that. I've also started to view the Bible's prohibitions in a new light. There are many things it advises against, and the simplistic notion that God sets these rules just because He can is nonsense. The reality is that if God warns us against certain behaviors, it's because He understands that they can cause harm to us or to others. God isn't just trying to assert authority; He is the authority. This was a huge shift in my thinking. I started to view things through the lens of God's love. My theology was now starting from that position. Everything was changing. Let me repeat that. God's prohibitions are there for our protection. Like a loving father he wants to protect us from harm and needless pain. You think about that for a bit.

Do I still pray? Do I still attend church? Honestly, I haven't been going as often as I used to. I'm not against church, but I have some simple prayers that I try to say daily, which you might find comforting too. The first one is: *O Heavenly King, Comforter, Spirit of Truth, who is everywhere and fills all things, the treasury of blessings and giver of life, come and dwell in us, cleanse us from every impurity, and save our souls.* This prayer is accessible to anyone, regardless of their faith—be it Judaism,

Christianity, Deism, Hinduism, Islam, or Buddhism. Another prayer I recite daily is the Our Father: *Our Father, who art in heaven, hallowed be thy name. Thy kingdom come; thy will be done on earth as it is in heaven. Give us this day our daily bread and forgive us our trespasses as we forgive those who trespass against us. Lead us not into temptation but deliver us from evil.* Remember, this prayer was given by Jesus, a Jewish rabbi, to His Jewish disciples. It's deeply rooted in Jewish tradition, yet Christians recite it daily. Lastly, I often pray simply throughout the day, saying, "Lord, have mercy." Whenever I see someone in distress on TV, someone being taken to the hospital, or witness a car accident, I quietly say to myself, "Lord, have mercy." King David expressed it well when he said, *"I cried unto the Lord, and He heard me from His holy hill."* Crying is one of the most powerful forms of prayer; tears cleanse the soul. God hears every tear offered in prayer. God is a loving heavenly father. If your experience with your earthly father has been painful, it can understandably affect how you perceive God. It's important to clarify this in your mind.

God's love for us is absolute, unwavering, and unconditional. It's time to start sowing the seeds of love in your life, knowing that you always reap what you sow. Embrace the belief in God's love for you and let that inspire you to show kindness and mercy to others. My life was transformed by God, and I know He can do the same for you. If you find yourself feeling broken, it's essential to seek healing before you can truly give it to others. Remember, hurt people often hurt others, and change is only possible if we take action. I hope that my story and this book motivate you to embark on or continue your journey toward wholeness. Don't let another day slip by. Seize the moment; it's your life, and you deserve to live it fully. God desires this for you, but you must align yourself with His grace.

Speaking of family, I must mention my mother. I had kept a relationship with her, albeit from a distance. However, after the recent fallout with my sister, I've come to terms with the fact that I may never see my mother again. I might have already seen my mother for the last time years ago when I returned from Israel. I made the decision to sever all contact with my sister. We were never close or had a normal relationship. As a result, my mother decided to stop talking to me again. She refuses to take my calls and has not called me back. If I meant anything to her, she would have called to ask what my side of the story was concerning my sister. I have come to terms with it all. I am not going to let them hurt me again. These are their decisions, and the onus is on them. I have closed this chapter in the book of my life. It's sad and unfortunate, but it is my reality. Instead of mourning the loss, I will celebrate the presence of my wife and children. I have great friends who care about me too. A lot of our misery comes from our inability to accept things as they are. We insist on things being the way we want them to be.

No family is without its flaws, unlike the picture-perfect ones we see on television. We must learn to appreciate what we have. My family includes my wife, my children, my aunt and uncle, and friends who feel like family. Not every chapter in our lives concludes with a happy ending, but that's just how life unfolds, right? It's time to stop wishing for something different and embrace reality. Make a firm decision to move forward, if necessary. Remember, you don't need anyone's approval to remove from your life anything or anyone that disrupts your peace or hinders your growth. This is your life, and it's your choice to shape it as you wish. I recognize that my health issues have shortened my lifespan. Honestly, with the way I feel, I

CHAPTER 10

don't have the desire to live another 20-30 years. I'm in pain, and it's challenging. I will strive to be the best husband, father, and friend I can be for however long I have left. Tomorrow is never guaranteed for any of us, regardless of our health or how well we care for ourselves. I view each day as a chance to make a positive impact on someone, whether through a chat or a social media post. Carpe diem, as they say. I understand that I've entered the winter of my life, and I've come to terms with it. I've embraced my role as the older, wiser individual that others seek guidance from. There's immense joy in uplifting others. I genuinely believe that whatever you possess, you should share. Whether it's wealth, wisdom, unique talents, or even just your time to visit someone who might be feeling isolated, give as much as you can. Trust me, what you give will return to you multiplied.

Now, let's talk about Jewish humor. The Jewish community has a rich tradition of humor, evident in the success of comedians from the Marx Brothers to Jerry Seinfeld. Humor serves as our survival mechanism, and no topic is too sensitive or off-limits. We embrace sarcasm and enjoy poking fun at one another in a lighthearted manner. I grew up watching Don Rickles, who had a knack for roasting everyone. His humor was harmless, and that was simply the norm back in those days. Indeed, this was a time before the world became overly sensitive, where people felt the need to be offended by everything, even when it wasn't warranted. My comedic style was influenced by my grandfather, Bill, who had a sharp wit. I often found that my unexpected remarks added an extra layer of humor.

Let me share a humorous memory from my time working in Kentucky back in 1997, a year filled with notable news events.

Now keep in mind that this is a group of very conservative Christians. One day, a group of us—about a dozen men—decided to grab lunch at a Chinese restaurant. After we finished eating, we lingered at the table, sharing laughs and stories. One guy, Dave, began reminiscing about his childhood hunting and fishing trips with his dad. He reached a point in his tale where he said, "My father always told me to eat anything I kill." Without missing a beat, I chimed in, "Jeffrey Dahmer's father said the same thing." The reactions were priceless—some were utterly shocked, while others were doubled over in laughter. I've always had a knack for quick comebacks and unexpected remarks, a talent I still possess today.

My wife often finds herself at a loss for words, but she can't help but laugh at my antics. I believe my sense of humor is one of the things she cherishes most about me, alongside my gentle nature. I thrive on the surprise and delight I see on people's faces when I make a bold joke. I genuinely love making others laugh, and I find immense joy in their laughter, often more than in my own. So, I encourage you to lighten up and not take yourself too seriously. The Bible says laughter is like medicine, and I wholeheartedly agree. In a world where political correctness and sensitivity seem to reign, many have lost their ability to laugh. I believe this contributes to the pervasive gloom and despair in our society. Where's the joy? Not for me! I'll stick to my roots, embracing laughter and seeking joy. Who wants to be around someone who's always downcast? Not me! I aspire to be someone others are drawn to.

Perhaps it's time for you to rediscover your laughter too. Remember, you don't need anyone's approval to find what brings you joy and purpose—this is your life to live!

As an adult once we recognize that a behavior is wrong, we

need to be accountable for our actions and change them. How to easily know a behavior is wrong is to ask yourself is this behavior harmful to others or myself? If it is, you need to change it. I developed a lot of bad behavior patterns during my adolescent years. I had to look at myself and understand why I was doing what I was doing. But I couldn't stop there. I had to go farther and make changes. I began to see where the influences came from and saw that the fruit of such behaviors was rotten to the core. As an adult you can't keep blaming your parents or others on your bad behavior. You are an adult, and you are making the choices now. Just as my children will have to move past the mistakes I made and the damage I caused them, everyone who desires to be whole must do the same. Do you just want to have an excuse and stay where you are, or do you want to move past it and be healed? It's up to you.

I developed certain pathologies as a young man that caused me to be a womanizer. I love Mick Hucknall of Simply Red and was listening to an interview with him recently. He grew up with his dad and had no maternal influence in his life. He became a womanizer as well. He reflected on his behavior and thought it might have been his attempt at receiving the love of a woman that was missing from his life. Maybe there was a sense of seeking female approval. Perhaps that was what I was doing too. I have had a very strained relationship with my mother since I was 12. We went decades without talking to each other. It was not a normal mother-son relationship, ever.

Epilogue

As we reach the end of our journey together, I hope you have received some encouragement. Our pain and failures are not meaningless as long as we learn from them and subsequently share our insights with others that they too may receive some hope and encouragement. At the heart of Judaism is the desire to make the world a better place—to leave things better than we found them. In Hebrew Tikkun Olam means (Fixing the World). Jews believe in actively repairing and improving the world. This concept, known as "Tikkun," encourages individuals to contribute positively to society, whether through acts of kindness, environmental stewardship and social justice. This is not to imply that other groups don't share these values. Jews were very active in the Civil Rights Movement in the Sixties. Famous American Rabbi Abraham Heschel, marched side by side with Martin Luther King Jr many times. Tikkun Olam is the main reason there are so many Jewish doctors. Jewish contributions to science and medicine have altered the course of history. Without always acknowledging it, the world is benefiting from Jewish contributions to medicine and technology on a daily basis. Statically, Jews are highly over represented in the fields of science and medicine. Jews are only 0.2% of the World's population but have been awarded over 20% of all Nobel Peace prizes. I am very proud of that accomplishment and contribution to the betterment of the

EPILOGUE

World.

I have left out many last names purposely, as I have no desire to embarrass anyone. I have left out many other stories to keep the size of the book manageable. I have included enough to give you an accurate overview of my life. I'm sure my sister and mother will take issue with what I've written but these are my memories and experiences. I've generally included the names of those who are presented in a favorable light. I've been blessed with many true friends over the years who loved and looked out for me, even when I didn't deserve it. May I be more like them.

I continue to face daily health challenges, including swallowing difficulties and reflux. Without a stomach or gallbladder and a pancreas that no longer functions, it's not always easy. I'm required to take enzyme replacement capsules with every meal. Additionally, I need special vitamins tailored for those who have undergone bariatric surgery or have similar intestinal issues. Unfortunately, I wasn't informed about these necessities when I left the hospital years ago, and none of my doctors advised me on them. For nearly five years, I battled fatigue and pain due to vitamin and mineral deficiencies. My godfather and dear friend Joe also faced stomach issues, which required surgery. About a year ago, he introduced me to these special bariatric vitamins. After starting them myself, I noticed a significant boost in my energy and overall well-being in less than a week. Back in 1979, I graduated high school weighing 179 lbs. In 2009 I hit my peak weight of 237 pounds. Because my training partner was a professional wrestler, many thought I was too. I certainly was big enough. I managed to shed 10 pounds, settling at an average of 227 for several years. By 2019, I dropped down to 136 pounds, and it was a struggle. Now, my weight has stabilized at 160 for the past few years, but I feel thin, weak, and low on energy at times. Despite this, I'm still fighting hard. My mind remains sharp, even if my body feels worn out.

Both of my kids are Millennials, born in 1988 and 1990, respectively. Like many in their age group, they seem to be off to a slower start in life than my generation, the Baby Boomers. I was disappointed for my son a few years ago, seeing him struggle to find his way. Now I realize I had a lot to do with that. If your child is struggling, make sure they know you may be disappointed *for* them but not disappointed *in* them. The difference between those feelings are huge. Your children want to please you. All children do, unless they have some emotional issue. It is crucial that your children hear from you that you love them and believe in them. They may never hear that from anyone else, so make sure they at least hear it from you.

Myself with Andrew and Randee

My daughter graduated cum laude from the University of Central Florida, and I see her doing great things with her life. We are so proud of her. My son is very bright as well. We may not have been perfect parents, but we did the best we could.

I had a very dysfunctional upbringing, and didn't have many positive examples to follow. Felicia didn't have the benefit of a father as he abandoned the family when she was an infant. Her mother was a positive force in her life however. What I am most proud of concerning my children is their compassion. A few months ago, after Monday Night RAW, they both stopped before I did to give money to a homeless person sitting on the very cold ground. I could only smile and thank God that they had turned out so well. With me as their father, it could have been different. God is gracious and merciful. They are intelligent, kind, and compassionate human beings. What more could a parent hope to raise?

Both of my children were good students and very well behaved growing up. They are kind and empathetic. I doubt it was easy growing up around me. Like my father, I was emotionally absent and distant. They were also witness to my outbursts of rage and anger. I would bottle up things until I'd explode. No doubt they were injured by emotional shrapnel flying towards them. I have deep regrets for the way I treated them in their early years.

If you are struggling with anything, ask for help. Whether it's a sin you want to stop, depression, anxiety, addiction, or something else, ask for help. Ask God, ask your Rabbi, Priest or Pastor, ask family, ask friends, ask doctors—just reach out. There is a lot of mental health counseling available. A simple Google search will display hundreds of available options. Stop suffering alone. If you have experienced trauma and grief, allow yourself to mourn. Talk about it, scream about it, let it all out. If you don't, that burden will affect every relationship you have, causing you to be a "stranger" wearing a mask. Listen to the Billy Joel song "The Stranger," it's profound. Until you face your past, your pain, your demons, you will never be your authentic self. You can become a great actor—I did. But at home, the mask I wore was a scowl. My son thought I hated him, and my wife always thought she had done something wrong. None of that was true. I was just carrying around pain and trauma that had never been dealt with. Once I finally faced my past, my wife said the scowl was gone.

Famous American author and Civil Rights advocate James Baldwin once said that *"not everything that is faced can be changed, but nothing is changed until it is faced."* The theme of facing our demons recurs in this story. It was not until I finally faced my own that the breakthrough happened for me. If you need professional help from a counselor, psychologist or psychiatrist to deal with your own demons, don't procrastinate any longer. You are valuable and deserve to be whole. Help is available. Resolve today that you will start on the path to make yourself better. It has been my experience that once the decision is made in your mind, you are halfway there towards your goal. You may not need professional help. You may just need to confess what has haunted you to a trusted friend. There is no one size fits all approach to healing and recovery. Just know that nothing changes if nothing changes. You need to resolve in your mind that you desire change.

What is most important is that you make the decision to be healed. There is a verse in the Gospel of John, chapter 5 verse 6, that always confused me. I quoted it in the foreword to the book. Jesus, who was healing all who came to him, approached a man who was crippled. He asked the man, *"Do you want to get well?"* Eventually I understood that not everyone who is broken whether emotionally or physically, wants to be get well. They don't want to be healed. Why? Their wound has come to identify who they are. It's how they see themselves and they can't see themselves any other way. Some seek pity and believe that no one will truly care about them if they were any other way than they are now. Oh the lies we tell ourselves. So the question still stands. Do YOU want to get well?

A word about drugs and alcohol: I used drinking and drugs to suppress my feelings and rage. In writing this book and reflecting on my behavior over the years I realize I had a bigger drinking problem than I thought I did. When I discovered kava and kratom, the desire for alcohol left. Kratom gave me a euphoric feeling that I liked—it tickles the opioid receptors of the brain. If you need to use kava to get off alcohol, go ahead, but try to wean yourself off it as soon as you can. The same goes for kratom. Many use kratom to get off heroin or other opioids. If it helps you get off those drugs, go ahead and use it, but realize you are trading one addiction for another. Try your best to wean off kratom as soon as possible. It is addictive and very expensive. This is not medical advice; I am sharing my experience with you. Kava has been used as a ceremonial drink for hundreds of years in Tonga and the Fijian Islands. I don't know the statistics, but I suspect they don't drink the same amount that Americans are consuming today. I have heard that Kava can affect your liver and there may be other negative effects. You may want to do your own research online and draw your own conclusions. Again, I offer no medical advice or opinions. These are just my personal experiences. The same holds true for Kratom. I have friends in the industry that swear by it and its benefits. I have not seen any negatives aside from addiction which is a big negative to me. The internet is filled with research; the pros and cons.

Recently I decided to stop drinking kava and kratom. I don't want to be addicted to anything. I don't drink alcohol anymore and gave up smoking in my Twenties. I am off opioids and the anti-anxiety medication I was on as well. I still take one antidepressant and a mood stabilizer at bedtime to help me sleep. I am a terrible sleeper. Always have been. I have had a few challenging moments over the last few months to test my resolve to be sober. I am a free man now. I am no longer a prisoner to drugs, alcohol or pain killers. My mind is clear. I can focus.

Never forget that God loves each and every one of us. The Bible says He desires the salvation of all people, and as we've previously discussed, salvation means being made whole. This is God's will for you. Satan desires to crush and destroy you. How we respond to challenges determines whose will is ultimately achieved God's or Satan's. The choice is ours. Please realize my theology is informed by the Judeo-Christian tradition. We believe in One all-powerful Creator God that created everything very good. Evil and sin entered the world through Satan (a personal malevolent being) that rebelled against God and wanted to be God. Satan deceived Adam and Eve and that brought a metaphysical change in God's good creation. God is all good and is love. Satan is our enemy and hates humankind and desires to destroy us. How do we determine if God or Satan is behind something? We look at the potential outcome. If it is for our good and well being, we know that God is behind it. If it will crush or destroy us, Satan is behind it. God will never do evil or tempt us to do evil. He cannot. It is against his nature. Now, I realize that not everyone reading this book subscribes to my theological worldview and that's fine. This is presented to give you a frame of reference to understand my views. My views have changed over the years. Not just my theology. My views on social issues including but not limited to the roles of women, LGBTQ issues, ecology, crime, punishment, politics, and more have changed. Change is a sign of growth. As we receive more information it should provoke us to reflect upon what we've been exposed to. We should think deeply about things. Just as a final thought, when I was young the Hippies in the Sixties were denounced by the establishment. I was exposed to the negative views of my family towards the anti-establishment Hippies. Now that I am much older and have had time to view our culture and especially our government, I can say with all certainty, the Hippies were right. There is a power structure that cares only for money and power and cares nothing about people. To acquire more money and power, they don't care how many people they harm. If you aren't familiar with the musical group Steely Dan, you should take a look at their album cover for *The Royal Scam*. It is brilliant and visually conveys what I am trying to write here.

While it is true that many others may have more material goods than you do, there are millions more people in the world who have less. Keep things in perspective and learn to be content. Discontentment leads to unhappiness. The apostle Paul said, *"learn to be content with such things that you have."* Much unhappiness and discontentment in the West derives from a gross materialism that values money and possessions over personal peace and internal well being. Always wanting more. Keeping up with the Joneses. The other side of the coin of contentment is gratitude. You cannot be content without gratitude. Being ungrateful is considered a sin in the bible. Keep in mind that God is not communicating that being ungrateful hurts his feelings. What is being communicated is that being ungrateful darkens your heart. It leads to unhappiness. If you are always wanting more, it's impossible to have peace in your heart at the same time.

Interestingly I recently learned that contentment is very important in Buddhism as well. I don't know much about Buddhism but in my studies of religions I recall learning that the Buddha taught the value of learning to let go of material possessions. Obviously, we need certain material things to function in this world, but I suppose the idea is to not be consumed with more and more just for mores sake. If you have more kids and need a bigger house, then get a bigger house. That is not a greed driven decision but a practical one.

When thinking about how to help others, use yourself as an example. "When this or that happened to me, this is what I did or how I responded," or, "I remember how I felt when this happened." When you do that, you will not raise their defenses, and they won't feel judged. Be humble and vulnerable. Your goal is not to make yourself look good but to help another person find freedom and healing. This book is an example of not making yourself look good. I seem like a real scoundrel. Well, I was. Those who have only known me in the past few years or so will find some of this story hard to believe. We are not our worst acts. We are who we choose to be. I am who I am now.

Follow the Light and experience the grace of God. The Bible says, "What does God require of you? To do justice, love mercy, and walk humbly with your God." Notice it says, "your God." You can know God for yourself, and He isn't hiding. Just call upon Him from your heart. He hears the cries of the brokenhearted and is near to them. God doesn't always give us answers, but He gives us something more important: Himself.

The bible also calls God, the God of Abraham, the God of Issac, and the God of Jacob. At first it's easy to miss the significance here. Each of the Patriarchs experienced God differently and personally. The only standard by which I would dare to judge someones experience with God would be their behaviors and attitudes. Are they now more loving and kind or hateful and destructive? I don't care what your mouth says. It's your actions that speak the loudest.

Be compassionate, kind, and merciful. Mercy is given to those who are merciful. Treat people well, whether they are cashiers, receptionists, or whatever. They are just trying to make it, like we all are. Treat the janitor the same as the owner of the company. Everyone deserves the same respect. A simple kind word and a smile can really bless their day.

The Bible says it's not good for man to be alone, and how true that is. I would not have survived my surgeries without the support and love of Felicia. She was by my side every day, loving me unconditionally since 1985. No matter what I put her through, she never stopped caring for me. The song "You make me feel Brand New" originally done by the Stylistics in 1974, and redone brilliantly by Mick Hucknall and Simply Red means a lot to me. I sent Mick Hucknall's rendition to Felicia while she was a work one day. She is the one who has restored me and makes me feel brand new. She is the hero of the story, my angel. I love her more each day. I hope you have or will find someone like her in your life.

I know I have made many terrible choices and mistakes in my life. There is a song by Linkin Park that my wife knows is important to me for obvious reasons. It's called "Leave out all the Rest." The chorus says, *"When my time comes, forget the wrong that I've done. Help me leave behind some reasons to be missed. Don't regret me, when you're feeling empty. Keep me in your memory, leave out all the rest."* I hope I have done some good while I was here.

I leave you with my three rules for better living, something I ask myself before I open my mouth:

1. Is it true?
2. Is it kind?
3. Is it necessary?

These simple rules will keep you out of trouble, and people will see you differently from others. Most people have tongues full of venom and love to gossip and tear others down. Don't be like that. Build others up. Love others as you want to be loved. Treat people as you want to be treated—the Golden Rule. I must confess that at times, I fail to follow my own rules. But I have a goal, a standard to reach for. When I fail, I resolve in my mind to do better next time. When I fall, I get right back up again. Don't stay down and don't get too down on yourself. Get up and keep going. We are looking for progress, not perfection.

If you want to feel right, do right. You want to feel good, do good. The great thing about the way the universe is designed is you don't need money to avail yourself of these laws built into it. The characters in films that I desire to emulate the most are those of exceptional moral character and integrity. I know that in my life I have not been a paragon of virtue and desperately desire to change that. I want to be known as a good man. I strive to be a man of honor and decency. Take some time to reflect on what changes you desire in your own life. How do you see yourself and how do others see you. Are you where you want to be? If not, what actions will you take to address that? The first step of change is the resolve to change. Making decisions is the hardest part. I have found that once I made a decision to change something about myself, I felt better about things even though the end result was still in the distance. Never underestimate the power of your resolve.

My main motivation for writing this book was to offer hope to hurting people. We are living through a terrible time in the world right now. So many are broken and losing hope. If I can reach a few people and offer them hope and help them to hang on a little longer, I have done the world a service. Every human being has value and purpose. The world would not be the same without you and I. We are all part of a much bigger picture. We often see ourselves as inconsequential but that isn't true. We are here for a purpose and that doesn't have to be front page news. Your kind words or smile can dissuade someone who was contemplating ending it all to hang on a little longer. Never minimize your importance in this world. Maybe someday in the future when all is revealed you will see how many lives you have saved and impacted without your even being aware of it.

Now, go change your life and start sowing the Seeds of Love

EPILOGUE

About the Author

Randy grew up in New Haven, Connecticut, in a middle-class Jewish family. From all outward appearances, his childhood seemed typical and happy. However, behind closed doors, things were not as they appeared. Deep emotional scars would affect his behavior for decades. His life and story provide a journey of self-discovery, enlightenment, healing, and hope. No matter how far off course you may feel, you can be restored and find the right path again. We are not defined by our worst actions; we are defined by who we choose to be in the present.

Randy is now retired and lives in Florida with his wife of many years, Felicia, and their cat, Charlie.

www.ingramcontent.com/pod-product-compliance
Lightning Source LLC
LaVergne TN
LVHW041810060526
838201LV00046B/1199